JOHN TAYLOR OF CAROLINE
PROPHETIC FOUNDING FATHER

John Taylor of Caroline c.1806

John Taylor of Caroline

PROPHETIC FOUNDING FATHER

JOSEPH R. STROMBERG

SHOTWELL
COLUMBIA · SO. CAR.
EST. 2015
PUBLISHING

Produced in the Republic of South Carolina by

SHOTWELL PUBLISHING LLC
Post Office Box 2592
Columbia, So. Carolina 29202
www.ShotwellPublishing.com

Cover: John Taylor of Caroline Portrait. Courtesy of wikimedia.com. Frontispiece: John Taylor of Caroline 1806. Courtesy of the National Portrait Gallery.

ISBN: 978-1-963506-25-9

FIRST EDITION

10 9 8 7 6 5 4 3 2 1

CONTENTS

Preface

JOSEPH STROMBERG is a historian whose research is both intense and wide. He tells it like it was. At the same time he gives us a broad historical sense of what the history means for our own times. And not in any trendy or superficial way.

John Taylor of Caroline County, Virginia, is arguably the most brilliant political thinker in the American experience. Writing in the earliest decades of the U.S. government, he clearly defined the Constitutional distortions and economic chicanery that were already laying the foundations of tyranny. Taylor saw our future: crony capitalism, judicial tyranny, limitless Presidential power, imperial government interfering with private society and foreign lands, taxation, catastrophic debt of a government that operates by shifting costs to future generations, bought Congressmen and bureaucrats.

Herein a model historian gives us the definitive treatment of a very important subject.

Clyde Wilson

Dutch Fork, South Carolina

Part I.

JOHN TAYLOR, REPUBLICANISM, LIBERTY, AND UNION

The Relevance of John Taylor

JOHN TAYLOR OF CAROLINE (1753-1824) has a secure, if minor, place in the history of American political thought. Charles A. Beard considered him "the philosopher and statesman of agrarianism" and "the most systematic thinker" of the Jeffersonian Republican party. Indeed, Beard's writing on Taylor, early in the 20th century, did much to revive interest in the Virginia polemicist.[1] Eugene T. Mudge, writing in 1939, saw Taylor's chief importance in his role as "prophet" of sectional struggle, and even civil war. English legal historian M.J.C. Vile sees Taylor as "in some ways the most impressive political theorist that America has produced." Gordon Wood writes that Taylor "brilliantly expressed the conception of American politics that had emerged from the revolutionary era..."[2] Avery Craven calls him "the most profound and the most persistent champion of individual and local democracy...." New

---

[1] Charles A. Beard, *Economic Origins of Jeffersonian Democracy* (New York: The Free Press, 1965 [1915]), 322.

[2] Gordon Wood, *The Creation of the American Republic, 1776-1787* (Chapel Hill, NC: University of North Carolina Press, 1969), 589.

1

Left historian William Appleman Williams once dismissed Taylor as "physiocrat" but later came to believe that Taylor "made the best case against empire as a way of life."[3]

Others have been less favorable. Louis Hartz faults Taylor for posing as a radical democrat, when Taylor ought to have tried to be the "American Disraeli."[4] The celebrated historian Richard Hofstadter calls Taylor "a provincial windbag" and seems aghast that Vernon Lewis Parrington found anything in Taylor worth his time.[5] For a liberal historian of Hofstadter's stamp, the views of Taylor and other Jeffersonian Republicans were entirely too "negative":

> The predominant strain in their economic thinking was laissez faire, their primary goal essentially negative — to destroy the link between the federal government and the investing classes. Acute and observant, their economic writing was at its best in criticism, but it offered no guide to a specific agrarian program. They had no plan; indeed, they made a principle of planlessness.[6]

And so, in time,

> ... Jeffersonian laissez faire became the political economy of the most conservative thinkers in the country. Fifty years after Jefferson's death, men like William Graham Sumner were writing sentences

---

3   Eugene T. Mudge, *The Social Philosophy of John Taylor of Caroline* (New York: Columbia University Press, 1939), 4; M.J.C. Vile, *Constitutionalism and the Separation of Powers* (Oxford: Clarendon Press, 1967), 167; Avery Craven, "John Taylor and Southern Agriculture," *Journal of Southern History* 4 (May 1938), 143; William Appleman Williams, *The Contours of American History* (Chicago: Quadrangle, 1966), 151-154, and *Empire as a Way of Life* (New York: Oxford University Press, 1980), 49.

4   Louis Hartz, *The Liberal Tradition in America* (New York: Harcourt, Brace & World, 1955), 119-121.

5   Richard Hofstadter, *The Progressive Historians: Turner, Beard, Parrington* (New York: Alfred A. Knopf, 1968), 413.

6   Richard Hofstadter, *The American Political Tradition* (New York: Vintage Books, n.d. [1948]), 37.

exactly like Jefferson's and John Taylor's to defend enterprising industrial capitalists and railroad barons from government regulation and reform.... William Jennings Bryan, leading the last stand of agrarianism as an independent political power, was still striving to give his cause the color or respectability by showing that, after all, the farmer too was a businessman![7]

There is much conflation in the passages just quoted, but for now suffice it to say that, first, Sumner saw himself as a critic and enemy of plutocracy; second, farmers certainly could be businessmen in the ordinary sense of the word.[8] As for capitalism — and Taylor's views of it — we shall get there soon enough. Writing in the same year, Manning Dauer managed to find in Taylor the father of "the present day agrarians, and also the present day states' rights industrialists."[9]

John Taylor's Life and Career

There have been a number of full-scale studies of Taylor. Older studies include those by William E. Dodd (1908), Henry Simms (1932), and Mudge (already mentioned). More recent are Robert E. Shalhope's *John Taylor of Caroline: Pastoral Republican* (1978) and C. William Hill's *Political Theory of John Taylor of Caroline* (1977).[10] An older study, to which I shall return, consists

---

7   Hofstadter, *American Political Tradition*, 39.

8   On Sumner and plutocracy, see H. A. Scott Trask, "William Graham Sumner: Against Democracy, Plutocracy, and Imperialism," *Journal of Libertarian Studies*, 18 (Fall 2004), 10-12; for American farmers' self-identification as businessmen, see William Appleman Williams, *Roots of the Modern American Empire* (New York: Random House, 1969), passim.

9   Manning Dauer, "Recent Southern Political Thought," *Journal of Politics*, 10 (May 1948), 328.

10   Robert E. Shalhope, *John Taylor of Caroline: Pastoral Republican* (Columbia, S.C.: University of South Carolina Press, 1980). C. William Hill, *The Political Theory of John Taylor of Caroline* (Cranbury, NJ: Associated University Presses, 1977). Two recent studies are Garrett Ward Sheldon and C. William Hill, Jr., *The Liberal Republicanism of John Taylor of Caroline* (Madison, NJ: Fairleigh Dickinson University Press, 2008), a promising attempt to sort out Taylor's ideological commitments, and Christopher Rühle, "Das politische Denken von John Taylor of Caroline" ["The Political Thought

of a two-part essay by Andrew Lytle, first published in 1924.[11] Despite this body of work, it seems fair to say that Taylor has been neglected relative to his actual merits.

John Taylor certainly met the requirements for an Old Dominion planter-statesman. Born to a good family, raised at the home of his uncle Edmund Pendleton, he attended William and Mary College, set up a law practice, served as a major in the Continental Army, and became a successful planter, owning several plantations and 150 slaves. Taylor preferred the quiet life of a country gentleman and devoted much time and energy to agricultural "reform" in his capacity as an applied agrarian, but did enter politics, at times, to defend free, republican society. Never a professional politician, he served in the Virginia legislature in 1779-81, 1783-85, and 1796-1800, and was appointed to fill out unexpired terms in the U.S. Senate in 1793-94, 1803, and 1822-24.[12]

This suggests that Taylor was not the sort of classical republican who professes to find freedom in political participation as such. But Taylor did put himself forward in a crisis, as witnessed by his apparent advocacy of secession and his sponsorship of the Virginia Resolutions, in the crisis set off by the Alien and Sedition Acts, the late 18th-century Patriot Act.[13]

---

of John Taylor of Caroline"] (PhD Dissertation, University of St. Gallen [Switzerland], 2007), which also looks very useful. [Since published as Christopher Rühle, *Das politische Denken von John Taylor of Caroline* (Bern: Haupt Verlag, 2010)— JRS].

11   Andrew Lytle, "John Taylor of Caroline," reprinted in M. E. Bradford, ed., *From Eden to Babylon: The Social and Political Essays of Andrew Nelson Lytle* (Washington, DC: Regnery/ Gateway, 1990), 45-76.

12   On Taylor's life and writings, see M. E. Bradford, "A Virginia Cato: John Taylor of Caroline and the Agrarian Republic," in John Taylor, *Arator*, M. E. Bradford, ed. (Indianapolis, Ind.: Liberty Classics, 1977), 11-46 (also in Bradford's *Reactionary Imperative* [Peru, Ill.: Sherwood Sugden & Company, 1990], 157-176; here I shall be citing the earlier publication).

13   On Taylor's readiness to secede, see Norman K. Risjord, *The Old Republicans* (New York: Columbia University Press, 1965), 14-15. Taylor worked in the Virginia assembly for passage of the Virginia Resolutions. Cf. Bradford, "A Virginia Cato," 23. For a short account of the Resolutions, see Lance Banning, *The Jeffersonian Persuasion: Evolution of a Party Ideology* (Ithaca, N. Y.: Cornell University Press, 1978), 264-266.

John Taylor's Writings

As one who always set himself against consolidated government, Taylor took an "Antifederalist" position during the debate over ratification of the constitution, as an associate of Patrick Henry's party in the Virginia ratifying convention. Not surprisingly, most of his political writing seeks to square Antifederalist principles with the constitution and to hold the victors to the promises about and understandings of the constitution, which they gave in the ratification debates.

With one notable exception, Taylor's works reflected immediate political battles of the day. His earliest essays attacked the Federalist funding system. His later works included reasoned polemics against the centralizing doctrines of both Congress and the Supreme Court. Taylor's magnum opus (the exception just mentioned), *An Inquiry into the Principles and Policy of the Government of the United States* (1814), which took him more than a decade to write, was a delayed reply to John Adams's *A Defence of the Constitutions of Government of the United States* (1787-88). Another work, *Arator* (1813, 1818), was a compilation of Taylor's newspaper articles on agricultural and political topics.[14] His last major works were *Tyranny Unmasked* (1822) and *New Views of the Constitution of the United States* (1823).

A typical Taylor book brings much learning and rhetoric to bear on a set of related issues, typically in the mode of jeremiad.[15] As befits a Christian, Taylor had a deep sense of the failings of human nature. At times, he seems quite Calvinist.[16] There are of course felicities and infelicities in Taylor's literary style. Writing to Thomas Jefferson on September 15, 1813, John Adams noted that he had received some unsigned printed pages in the mail. "The Conclusion of the whole is that an Aristocracy of Bank Paper,

---

14　For bibliographies of Taylor's writings, see Mudge, *Social Philosophy of John Taylor*, and Hill, *Political Theory of John Taylor of Caroline* (Cranbury, NJ: Associated University Presses, 1977).

15　On the "republican jeremiads" of John Taylor," see Robert E. Shalhope, "Toward a Republican Synthesis," *William & Mary Quarterly*, 29 (January 1972), 63.

16　See, e.g., John Taylor of Caroline, *Tyranny Unmasked* (Indianapolis: Liberty Fund, 1992 [1822]), 265-268.

is as bad as the Nobility of France or England. I, most assuredly, will not controvert this point, with this man. Who he is, I cannot conjecture. The Honourable John Taylor of Virginia, of all men living or dead first Occurred to me." In reply, on October 18, 1813, Jefferson commented that the author of the unsigned "pamphlet on aristocracy... may be known from the quaint, mystical and hyperbolical ideas, involved in affected, new-fangled and pedantic terms, which stamp his writings." Adams wrote in reply on November 12, "The style answers every characteristic, that you have intimated." Yet there was "a great deal of good Sense in Arator. And there is some in his 'Aristocracy.'"[17] John Randolph of Roanoke thought Taylor's *Inquiry* very good but cried, "For heaven's sake, get some worthy person to do the second edition into *English*."[18]

Taylor's sometimes difficult style detracts only slightly from books well worth reading. Often there are interesting compressions and apt expressions. And Taylor's work provides welcome relief from James Madison's Latinate and periodic sentences. Indeed, Taylor resembles William Faulkner in that his work is sometimes better understood when read aloud, for Taylor was both a rhetor and a preacher. He was aware of complaints about his writing. He ends the preface to *Tyranny Unmasked*, as follows: "As to its style, it is dictated by a wish to be understood by every reader. The writer has not an ability to angle for fame with the bait of periods; nor a motive for consulting a temporary taste, by a dish of perfumes."[19] Finally, Taylor's semantic/semiotic turn bears noting — his interest in the abuses of "artificial phraseology" and counterfeit words aping the real ones. Historian Robert Shalhope has remarked on Taylor's "perceptiveness" in this regard.[20]

---

17   Lester J. Cappon, ed., *The Adams-Jefferson Letters* (New York: Simon and Schuster, 1971), 376, 392, 394.

18   John Randolph quoted in Michael O'Brien, *Conjectures of Order: Intellectual Life and the American South, 1810-1860, II* (Chapel Hill, NC: University of North Carolina Press, 2004), 796.

19   Taylor, *Tyranny Unmasked*, xxix.

20   John Taylor of Caroline, *Construction Construed and Constitutions Vindicated* (New York: Da Capo Press, 1970 [1820]), 201 ("artificial phraseology"); Shalhope, *John Taylor*, 75.

Taylor as an Impractical Politician

Taylor was not much of a practical politician. He worked best as a critic trying to keep the public, and indeed his own party, honest. His attacks on the entrenched Federalists included pieces written under the pen name "Franklin" in the mid-1790s in Oswald's *Independent Gazetteer*.[21] Pamphlets like An *Examination of the Late Proceedings Congress Respecting the Official Conduct of the Secretary of the Treasury* (1793), *An Enquiry into the Principles and Policy of Certain Public Measures* (1794). *A Definition of Parties* (1795) and *An Argument Respecting the Constitutionality of the Carriage Tax* (1795) followed. Banning sees these minor works as "probably the most important source for an understanding of Republican thought in the middle 1790s."[22] Certainly, we can see in them the beginnings of Taylor's mature system of thought.

Perhaps the worst tragedy that can befall a set of principles is to have a political party professing allegiance (however false) to them, come to power. We have seen this in our days with "conservatism." And so, it probably was with Jeffersonian republicanism.

Certainly, the luminous Henry Adams and the contemporary historian Forrest McDonald tax Jefferson's party with failures allegedly stemming from a too-rigid adherence to republican ideas. Taylor, Randolph, and the Quids drew a different conclusion.[23] It is worth pointing out here that while Taylor's writings exercised an ongoing influence on Jefferson's views, Jefferson was more open to Taylor's ideas when out of power.[24]

In 1801-1802, with the aid of a committee in Caroline County headed by his uncle Edmund Pendleton, Taylor promoted "amendments restricting the powers of the government in regard to the army, the navy, finances, and the making of treaties."

---

21   Banning, *Jeffersonian Persuasion*, 237.

22   Banning, 193.

23   See Norman K. Risjord, *The Old Republicans: Southern Conservatism in the Age of Jefferson* (New York: Columbia University Press, 1965).

24   See Robert E. Shalhope, "Thomas Jefferson's Republicanism and Antebellum Southern Thought," *Journal of Southern History*, 42 (November 1976), 548-551.

As late as 1804, he could still write *A Defense of the Measures of the Administration of Thomas Jefferson*. But discontent within Republican ranks had begun and John Randolph went into opposition in 1806. This was the beginning of the so-called Quids as a minority Republican opposition. In 1810, Taylor gave his reasons: he saw the republican split as resulting from the administration's compromise between republican and federalist policies.[25]

Along with Randolph and a few others, Taylor opposed the War of 1812 — his own party's war — calling it "this metaphysical war..."[26] An account set down much later records an exchange between Taylor and war hawk John Roane Jr.:

> Once, during the War of 1812, he beat John Taylor, of Caroline, for Congress, and in one of the conflicts at the Bowling Green, Taylor's own stronghold, Taylor, who opposed the war said: "But Mr. Roane, the taxes, sir, the taxes."
>
> "Well, sir; the taxes, what of them? I do not fear taxes, nor do the people. They want freedom; they don't want money."
>
> "How high would you tax for this war?"
>
> "I would tax them, sir, ten cents in the dollar."
>
> "Suppose, sir, that should be insufficient?"
>
> "Then, sir, I would tax them twenty cents in the dollar."
>
> "But suppose they would not stand it?"
>
> "Then, sir, I would not ask them. I would tax them thirty, forty, fifty, sixty, seventy, eighty, ninety, one hundred cents in the dollar. Col. Taylor, I would

---

25   Risjord, *Old Republicans*, 24-25.

26   On Taylor's opposition to the war, see Risjord, 149-150.

tax the shirts off the peoples' backs and make them free, whether they would or not. What is your next bugbear?"[27]

Evidently, such war hawk bombast proved popular with the voters. Andrew Lytle describes the period as follows:

> Jefferson had hamstrung himself with the all-Federalist-all-Republican doctrine.... In trying to keep the ship of state afloat during squalls from foreign parts, Jefferson and Madison neglected domestic principles, until dissension spread into mutiny. The embargoes and later the War of 1812 ruined New England's shipping and turned her capital towards manufacturing. At the conclusion of hostilities the factories demanded protection. The depleted currency and the debt contracted to prosecute the war made the richest ground for patronage, a National Bank, and the sectional taxation of the Southern planter and farmer.[28]

The war strengthened the standing army and "discredited" the militia — by showing it was not useful for invading Canada, even if it might be adequate for local defense. Wartime monetary expansion by the new bank led to the Panic of 1819[29] and in this context a Congressional Committee report arguing for expanded protectionism, a suggestion which drew forth Taylor's *Tyranny Unmasked* (1822).

---

27   Letter of Frank Gildart Ruffin, June 1, 1870, in [unsigned: presumably Lyon Gardiner Tyler], "The Roane Family," *William and Mary Quarterly Historical Magazine*, 18 (April 1910), 274.

28   Lytle, "The Backwoods Progression," in *From Eden to Babylon*, 84.

29   Murray N. Rothbard's *Panic of 1819* (New York: Columbia University Press, 1963) remains the best account of the panic, its economic and political consequences, as well as the stimulus it gave to American economic thinking.

Ideological Background of Taylor's Writings

This brings us, alas, to the Forty Years War in American Historiography between the paladins of the "republican school" and the defenders of a "liberal" American Revolution and founding. J.G.A. Pocock, a prime mover of the republican school, sees classical republicanism (also "civic humanism" or "country ideology") as the essence of English Opposition thought. This outlook, radically opposed to liberalism, descended from Nicolò Machiavelli through James Harrington and the Commonwealthmen into the American Revolution. It centered on such categories as court vs. country, mixed constitutions, balanced orders, and independent, armed, agrarian proprietors as bulwark and defenders of the state.[30] Further, these ideas came over to America in two bread streams — from Henry St. John Bolingbroke and his allies and from a more "bourgeois" group of Radical Whigs. Both tendencies fought the state-financial revolution which, by means of monetized public debt, made possible standing armies, necessitated higher taxes, and supported absolute monarchy.

Historians tend to lump all such figures together as agrarians "nostalgically" resisting expanded commerce. This interpretation can be quite misleading.[31] As Isaac Kramnick writes: "One can be both a bourgeois radical and a thinker concerned with themes important to the civic humanist tradition."[32] On the republican school's reading, John Locke was out as the main influence on the American thought of the 1770s and after.

---

30   On all these points, see J.G.A. Pocock, *The Ancient Constitution and the Feudal Law* (Cambridge: Cambridge University Press, 1957), "Machiavelli, Harrington, and English Political Ideologies in the Eighteenth Century," *William & Mary Quarterly*, 22 (October 1965), 549-83, and *Machiavellian Moment* (Princeton: Princeton University Press, 1975), *passim*.

31   See Isaac Kramnick, *Bolingbroke and His Circle* (Cambridge: Harvard University Press, 1968), *passim*, and "English Middle Class Radicalism in the Eighteenth Century," *Literature of Liberty*, 3 (Summer 1980), 32-33.

32   Kramnick, "English Middle Class Radicalism," 32-33.

Republican Revolution

But certainly, American revolutionary Whig ideology drew on liberal, Lockean notions of self-ownership, natural law, and natural rights. American Whigs appealed to the "rights of Englishmen" and employed classical republican ideas as well. These ideas, combined and cross-fertilized, constituted what Bernard Bailyn calls a "transforming ideology."[33] American Whigs evidently fused several compatible ideologies into a reasonably coherent libertarian/ republican *Weltanschauung* informing the American Revolution.

Radical Whigs on both sides of the Atlantic viewed power as inherently expansionist: only constant public vigilance could keep liberty safe. They took British imperial policies after 1763 as proving an intention to use standing armies and taxes to subvert liberty. To the former threat, American ideologists posed militias as the viable alternative.[34] In Bernard Bailyn's view, the themes of Country vs. Court and Liberty vs. Power fell completely together, leading Americans to take "a negative view of government" and to see "the rulers and the ruled" as antagonistic forces.[35]

We may concede the coexistence of various political "languages" without prejudging the main commitments of the American Revolution.[36] Luigi Marco Bassani has written an interesting autopsy for the unrepentant republican school of historians and

---

33   On Lockeanism, see C. B. Macpherson, *The Political Theory of Possessive Individualism* (Oxford: The Clarendon Press, 1962); and John Locke, *Two Treatises of Government,* ed. Peter Laslett (New York: New American Library, 1965), esp. Laslett's introduction. On the American revolutionary synthesis, see Bernard Bailyn, *Ideological Origins;* Shalhope, "Towards a Republican Synthesis"; H. Trevor Colbourn, *The Lamp of Experience* (Chapel Hill, N.C.: University of North Carolina Press, 1965); Forrest McDonald, "A Founding Father's Library," *Literature of Liberty* I (January-March 1978), 4-15; Murray N. Rothbard, "Modern Historians Confront the American Revolution," *Ibid.,* 16-41; and Pauline Maier, *From Resistance to Revolution* (New York: Alfred A. Knopf, 1972).

34   See William F. Marina, "Revolution and Social Change: The American Revolution as a People's War," *Literature of Liberty,* I (April-June 1978), 21-27.

35   Shalhope, "Towards a Republican Synthesis," 64-65.

36   For one thing, the Americans simply did not have the word "liberal" as an ideological label; they did have "republican."

we may leave the historians' Forty Years War to one side.[37] I merely note the sheer ethereality of some republican school writers and the absence of materially motivated actors in their work.[38]

Confederation, Constitution, and Union

Within a few years of the victory of the revolution, a group of centralizing Whigs sought to replace the Articles of Confederation with a new constitution capable of undergirding an American mercantilist political economy.[39] The ratification debates unleashed old themes, as the misnamed Antifederalists attacked the constitution as a betrayal of the Revolution. At the same time, the misnamed Federalists (nationalists) restated republicanism and tried to annex popular sovereignty to the projected central government.[40]

The centralizers prevailed and governed until 1800. Their opponents gradually organized under the name of Republicans and broadly continued the Antifederalist cause.[41] The Federalists found their mercantilist policies — the National Bank, excises, redemption of wartime certificates, standing army, and tariffs — assailed by the Republicans in a replay of English debates after

---

37   Luigi Marco Bassani, "The Bankruptcy of the Republican School," *Telos*, 124 (Summer 2002), 131-157.

38   Consider, for example, J.G.A. Pocock, who, in a nuanced and interesting treatment of Edmund Burke's views on paper money in the French Revolution, cannot be bothered even to hint whether or not Burke was right about what he said. J.G.A. Pocock, "The Political Economy of Burke's Analysis of the French Revolution," in *Virtue, Commerce, and History* (Cambridge, MA: Cambridge University Press, 1985), 193-212.

39   For James Madison, "father of the Constitution," as a mercantilist thinker, and on the Constitution as "a feudal and mercantilist instrument of government," see Williams, *Contours of American History*, 157-162.

40   Wood writes that Federalists sought to "retard the thrust of the Revolution with the rhetoric of the Revolution," thereby inventing "a distinctly American political theory but only at the cost of eventually impoverishing later American political thought" (*Creation of the American Republic*, 562). They could do this only by way of the vague, unempirical, and unhistorical theorem that a Single American People existed; for two refutations out of many, see Abel P. Upshur, *A Brief Inquiry into the True Nature and Character of Our Federal Government* (New York: Da Capo Press, 1971 [1840]), and Kevin Carson, "Chapter 1: The Original Source of Sovereignty" (2003), at http://www.mutualist.org/id21.html .

41   On the overlapping of Antifederalists and Republicans, see Jackson Turner Main, *The Anti-Federalists* (Chapel Hill, N.C.: University of North Carolina Press, 1961), 281, and Beard, *Economic Origins of Jeffersonian Democracy*. Similarly, former Tory areas tended to become Federalist strongholds: Marina, "Revolution and Social Change," 35.

1688. The parallels were in fact close, and John Taylor did his part in underscoring them. In his assaults on the Federalists' funding system, Taylor can be seen as "an American Bolingbroke, speaking for an American 'Country' party." As Pocock puts it, Taylor wrote "anti-Hamiltonian polemics in which the ghosts of Swift and Bolingbroke stalk on every page."[42]

---

42   Banning, *Jeffersonian Persuasion*, 200-201. J.G.A. Pocock, *The Machiavellian Moment: Florentine Political Thought and the Atlantic Republican Tradition* (Princeton, NJ: Princeton University Press, 1975), 531.

Part II.

John Taylor on
Federal and Constitutional Questions

Liberalism

TAYLOR STOOD ON LIBERAL GROUND in holding that men were a mixture of good and evil. Self-interest was the only real constant in human action.[43] He broke with archaic-republican ideas of mixed constitutions and social balance. His key idea was to *divide power up* so many ways, federally and departmentally, that no set of officials possessed enough of it to overawe the government or the people. This goes far beyond the tame notions of "checks and balances" and "separation of powers."

The end of government was the protection of men's lives, liberty, and justly acquired property. Government rested on the "natural, individual right of self government," not on social contract.[44] By denying conventional social contract theory, Taylor avoided the implication that people *surrender* natural rights by a compact among themselves or with their "rulers" or institutions. If anything, this makes Taylor more radical than Locke and brings him closer to Thomas Paine, whom the neo-Aristotelian philosopher John Wild saw as a better exponent of natural law than Locke.[45] Instead, sovereignty resulted from men's living together in a community,

---

43   Mudge, *Social Philosophy of John Taylor*, 10-12.

44   Mudge, 57.

45   John Wild, *Plato's Modern Enemies and the Theory of Natural Law* (Chicago: University of Chicago Press, 1953), 120-123.

and this sovereignty organized the protection of the individual. True to his Antifederalist origins, Taylor located sovereignty — the ultimate right of self-government — in the peoples of the states, or "state-nations" and not in a fancied, single people of the United States in the aggregate.[46] For Taylor, the state governments were already good enough. He was far more concerned with the problem of dividing and taming central power through federalism.

Federalism

Merrill Peterson writes that "Taylor, with a hard knot of Virginia Republicans, had never overcome the Anti-Federalist dogma on the Constitution. Wrong in essential principles, the compact necessarily produced vicious effects, as in the centralized privilege and corruption of the Hamiltonian system, and no mere change of men or of party could set the government aright."[47] Indeed, Taylor wrote that, at the constitutional convention, there had been a "monarchical" school (represented by Hamilton) and a "consolidating" school (represented by Madison), but that their opponents had kept both somewhat within bounds.[48]

In an age rife with half-digested social contract theory,[49] Taylor was rather uninterested in "social contract" at the level of the states. He took the states as *given* and discussed how *they* had contracted with one another to create a limited union under certain rules, with a common agent. These rules were, for Taylor, "political law," setting structural, procedural, and substantive restraints on power.

---

46   For empirical support of Taylor's views, see Henry B. Dawson, "The Motley Letter," *Historical Magazine*, 2nd ser., IX (March 1871), 157-201, Claude H. Van Tyne, "Sovereignty in the American Revolution," *American Historical Review* 12 (April 1907), 529-545, and Merrill Jensen, *The Articles of Confederation* (Madison: University of Wisconsin Press, 1966), 161-176.

47   Merrill D. Peterson, *Thomas Jefferson and the New Nation* (New York: Oxford University Press, 1970), 610-611.

48   John Taylor of Caroline, *New Views of the Constitution of the United States* (Washington, DC: Regnery Publishing, Inc., 2000 [1823]), 256-257. See M. E. Bradford, "The Constitutional Convention as Comic Action," in *Original Intentions: On the Making and Ratification of the United States Constitution* (Athens, GA: University of Georgia Press, 1993), 1-16.

49   Today, it is Straussians, who profit from the confusion. See Ronald J. Pestritto and Thomas G. West, eds., *The American Founding and the Social Compact* (New York: Lexington Books, 2003), for a compendium of these fables.

Taylor had to break new ground in order to achieve the goals of *American* republicanism. In so doing, he opened up a Southern front against James Madison's theory of the union.[50]

According to historian Michael Kammen, however, Southern politicians and publicists willfully and wickedly misrepresented the ideas of Madison. Thus, William Giles and John C. Calhoun attached to Madison, the Father of the Constitution, certain views on states rights, secession, and the like, hoping thereby to gain prestige for their nefarious, new-fangled readings of that instrument. In other words, they *lied* about Madison's real views, views naturally more authoritative than their own.[51] There is also the related allegation — from other sources — that Calhoun opposed public funding for the printing of Madison's journal of the Constitutional Convention out of "fear" that the document would overthrow his (Calhoun's) "theory" of the union.[52]

But the answer to these claims is that Madison's views existed in some flux and that in confusing different audiences Madison managed to confuse himself. To the extent that Madison had a consistent view of the nature of the union, it was indeed different from that of the Virginia School — Taylor, Roane, and (sometimes) Jefferson — and their successors. The latter knew full well that Madison was *unreliable* on the fundamentals.[53]

Allegedly "new" views of the constitution were needed precisely because Madison and his allies had made a complete muddle of all the important questions. They intended (one supposes) that their conscious obfuscations would protect the public mind from unnecessary worry, giving the "new paper" a chance to work. It

---

50   See Taylor, *New Views*, 72-74.

51   Michael Kammen, *A Machine That Would Go of Itself: The Constitution in American Culture* (New York: Alfred A. Knopf, 1986), 55-57.

52   See Burton J. Hendrick, *Bulwark of the Republic: A Biography of the Constitution* (Boston: Little, Brown & Co., 1937), 261-264.

53   Cf. Albert Taylor Bledsoe, *Is Davis a Traitor, or Was Secession a Constitutional Right Prior to the War of 1861?* (Richmond, VA: The Hermitage Press, 1907; reprint: Wiggins, Miss.: Crown Rights Book Co., n.d.), 2-4, 174-177.

was left to Taylor to unravel these knots. Later, as the questions became more pressing, Calhoun entered the fray to address the problems created by the Federalists' artful dodging.[54]

For many of the framers, the U.S. constitution was *sui generis*: somehow providing a confederation and at the same time a true national state. Madison wrote that ratification was "the act of the people, as forming so many independent States, not as forming one aggregate nation,"[55] but such language seems to have been a sop to the "fears" of opponents. In the famous Tenth Federalist, Madison inverted the traditional view, pressed by Antifederalists, that a government on a grand scale could not remain republican, and asserted that to "extend the sphere" actually solved the problem of "faction." But an expanded (and expanding) union to dilute and alleviate faction presupposed, as Williams observes, an American mercantilism. By tying republican liberty to territorial expansion Madison long anticipated Turner's frontier thesis and read a kind of imperial logic into the constitution.[56]

Madison's political science dodged substantive questions of ultimate power and the actions of the first Congress under the new "paper" began the refutation of Madison's optimistic theorem. By contrast, Taylor hoped for divisions of, and limits on, power to cut off organized state favoritism, which was the cause and instrument of faction.[57] A well-ordered republic need not expand

---

54   See discussion below on Taylor's *New Views*. And see Clyde N. Wilson, "Little Jimmy's Last Hurrah," in *From Union to Empire: Essays in the Jeffersonian Tradition* (Columbia, SC: Foundation for American Education, 2003), 66-69.

55   Alexander Hamilton, John Jay, and James Madison, *The Federalist* (New York: The Modern Library, 1937), No.9, 50-53, and No. 39, 246-247. The terms were Montesquieu's — the conclusions were not.

56   Williams, *Contours of American History*, 160, and James Madison, Federalist No. 10, any edition. Political scientists David P. Calleo and Benjamin M. Rowland write: "the Madison of the *Federalist Papers* did not advocate constant expansion — only a base large enough at the outset to make it difficult for a single majority faction to form itself and control the state." *America and the World Economy: Atlantic Dreams and National Realities* (Bloomington: Indiana University Press, 1973), 280 note. Even so, Madison's audience — including the later Madison — adopted ongoing expansion as a central theorem of republicanism as they understood it.

57   Grant McConnell, "John Taylor and the Democratic Tradition," *Western Political Quarterly*, 4 (March 1951), 27. On the overthrow of Madison's theorem, see William Maclay, *The Journal of William Maclay* (New York: Frederick Ungar, 1965 [1927; 1890]). Maclay served as a Senator for Pennsylvania in the first Congress.

to prevent faction. That course was unwise, in any case. Empire would undermine liberty through war, armies, debt, and taxes — the whole array of anti-republican (Court) policies. Mercantilism and empire ran in the same stream.[58]

Competing Pieces of Government

John Taylor opposed unalloyed sovereignty and upheld the Antifederalist position that self-government rested, finally, with the peoples of the several states, who by a new "political law" had delegated the exercise of certain powers to a general *agent*, itself not sovereign.[59] *In extremis,* the natural right of self-defense permitted state interposition (nullification) to oppose federal usurpations. As a last resort, secession was both a constitutional and revolutionary remedy.

Divisions of Power

Taylor supposed the states to possess full concurrent juris-diction with the federal government, hence his strenuous attack on John Marshall's decision denying Maryland the right to tax the National Bank (*McCulloch v. Maryland,* 1819). Taylor de-nied that Supreme Court decisions set binding precedents for the state courts to follow. They applied at most between the parties to the particular case. Taylor admitted the possibility of differing constructions of the same constitutional provisions but saw such an outcome as better than allowing the Court to rewrite the con-stitution at will. The Supreme Court's "usurpation" of final inter-pretive say would effectively transfer sovereignty to the general government. Mudge sees Taylor's system as "a *laissez faire* notion applied to the elements of government" and M.J.C. Vile calls it a "fantastic picture of a fragmented governmental system" with the

---

58   Cf. Bradford, "A Virginia Cato," 26-27.

59   In its treaties with Cuba (1903, 1934) and Panama (1903) regarding, respectively, Guantanamo Bay and the Canal Zone, the US government belatedly discovered that another contracting sovereign state can indeed delegate the exercise of powers to an agent or partner, which will wield them "as if" it were the sovereign — a position it deemed absurd and treasonous in 1861.

"virtue [of] consistency." William Grampp characterizes it as "the most extreme extension made in America of the idea of a minimum state."[60]

Spheres of Action Without Sovereignty in the Spheres

In his *Inquiry* (1814), Taylor writes that political law is meant to control all representatives and agents. The people retain ultimate rights over the system, despite "the doctrine that this power, having thought and spoken once, had lost the right of thinking and speaking forever"[61] — precisely the nationalist and Straussian view of the "founding." Taylor continues: "If a sovereign power, by one declaration of its will, does not lose its sovereignty, it must retain also an unlimited freedom, in whatever is necessary towards any future declaration of its will; otherwise its first will, must be its last will." In the federal union, "The people of the states, treated and united as independent of each other, surrendered a portion of their independent rights, into a common treasury, and retained another portion. The contract derives its force, not from the consent of a majority of the states, but from the separate consent of each."[62] Thus, if a minority of the Senate should block a much-wanted constitutional amendment, the states might call "a convention; the result of which any one state may refuse to concur in, because each state will resume its original right to refuse or consent, as being independent of each other in negotiating the terms of a new union."[63]

---

60   Mudge, *Social Philosophy of John Taylor,* 93; Vile, *Constitutionalism,* 172; and William Grampp, "John Taylor: Economist of Southern Agrarianism," *Southern Economic Journal,* 11 (January 1945), 257.

61   John Taylor of Caroline, *An Inquiry into the Principles and Policy of the Government of the United States* (London: Routledge & Kegan Paul, 1950 [1814]), 424.

62   Taylor, *Inquiry,* 424, 444.

63   Taylor, *Inquiry,* 445.

Construction Construed

Taylor's *Construction Construed* (1820) throws more light on these matters. The book's immediate target was John Marshall's decision in *McCulloch v. Maryland* (1819). Taylor writes that, "The unknown powers of sovereignty and supremacy may be relished, because they tickle the mind with hopes and fears...." Further, "the term 'sovereignty,' was sacrilegiously stolen from the attributes of God, and impiously assumed by Kings. Though they committed the theft, aristocracies and republicks have claimed the spoil." In any case, the "idea of investing servants with sovereignty, and that of investing ourselves with a sovereignty over other nations, were equally preposterous."[64] (Now of course "we" do both.)

This was because "Sovereignty is neither fiduciary nor capable of limitation." In North America, we had concluded that sovereignty had been the "root" of oppression, despotic power, and "pecuniary fanaticism." We therefore meant "to eradicate it by establishing governments invested with specified and limited powers." Thus, under our systems, "the people or the states retain all the powers they have not bestowed" and "ungranted rights remain also with the grantors, but these are the people."[65] This "canon" of constitutional interpretation, by which powers "not granted" are actually taken to be *not granted*, or nonexistent, failed to impress John Marshall and the founders of Harvard Law School[66]; or, to the extent it impressed them, they found ways around it. And yet it set a certain standard.

---

64   Taylor, *Construction Construed*, 25-26.

65   *Ibid.*, 27-28, 37. For a good example of "pecuniary fanaticism," see Thomas E. Kaiser, "Money, Despotism, and Public Opinion in Early 18th-Century France: John Law and the Debate on Royal Credit," *Journal of Modern History*, 63 (March 1991), 1-28.

66   R. Kent Newmyer, "Harvard Law School, New England Legal Culture, and the Antebellum Origins of American Jurisprudence," *Journal of American History*, 74 (December 1987), 814-835.

Means and Ends, Ends and Means, and So On

Taylor wished to sideline the whole rhetoric of sovereignty. In his view, Americans had never bought that tired old horse. With respect to Marshall's method for turning means into new powers, he says:

> Previously to our revolutionary war, the colonies had been thoroughly lectured upon the subjects of sovereignty, supremacy, and a division of powers.... The parliament contended, that the right of making war, conceded by the colonies, implied a right of using all the means necessary for obtaining success; such as raising a revenue, appointing collectors, raising troops, quartering them upon the colonies, and many other internal laws; and that the right of regulating commerce, also involved a right of imposing duties, and establishing custom houses for their collection; arguing, that it would be absurd to allow powers, and with-hold any means necessary or proper for their execution. *The colonies replied, that it would be more absurd to limit powers, and yet concede unlimited means for their execution....*[67]

The last sentence goes to the heart of the thing.

Taylor continues,

> ... [T]he doctrine of absolute sovereignty, with its indefinite catalogue of appendances, can adduce in its defence many plausible arguments, and enumerate sundry conveniences which might result, from its unlimited capacity to devote both persons

---

67   Taylor, *Construction Construed*, 53 (emphasis supplied).

and property to whatever purposes it may think proper. What conveniences may arise from the absolute subordination appertaining to it, in war![68]

But this seemed to have little to do with the actual constitution: "If congress possessed an unlimited power to appropriate the publick money raised by taxes, there was no occasion to specify the objects to which it might be applied, such as to raise and *support* armies, to provide and *maintain* a navy."[69]

If we were to follow Marshall's lead, "As ends may be made to beget means, so means may be made to beget ends, until the co-habitation shall rear a progeny of unconstitutional bastards, which were not begotten by the people...." Great chains of reasoning would lead to such conclusions as these: "Roads are necessary in war; therefore congress may legislate locally concerning roads." In the same way, horses being even more essential for war, "an implied power of legislation, will certainly invest congress with a legislative power over horses."[70] (Marshall had cited the war power as one possible source of an *implied* power to charter the Bank of the United States.[71])

In Taylor's view, Americans had never signed on for the international jurists' theories of absolute, unitary sovereignty, from which such deductions were made. Instead, they had instituted strictly limited governments that were their mere trustees or agents.[72] Thirteen such peoples had by contract created a common agent for certain limited ends. Sovereignty in the European or Blackstonian sense need never come into it.

Here is how Taylor framed the problem. Asking how governments became unrestrained tyrannies, he writes:

---

68   *Ibid.*, 76.

69   *Ibid.*, 75.

70   *Ibid.*, 84, 170.

71   John Marshall, *McCulloch v. Maryland*, in Henry Steele Commager, ed., *Documents in American History*, I (New York: Appleton-Century-Crofts, 1963), 213–220.

72   Taylor, *Construction Construed*, 27–28, 31–38, 280, 286–289.

To answer this question, turn your eyes towards a government accoutred in the complete panoply of fleets, armies, banks, funding systems, pensions, bounties, corporations, exclusive privileges; and in short, possessing the absolute power to distribute property, according to the pleasure, the pride, the interest, the ambition, and the avarice of its administrators; and consider whether such a government is the servant or the master of the nation. However oppressive, is it not able to defy, to deride and to punish the complaints of the people? Partisans, purchased and made powerful by their wealth, zealously sustain the abuses by which their own passions are gratified. I discern no reason in the principles of our revolution, for investing our governments which such of these instruments for oppression, as were both unnecessary for the end in view, and even inimical to its attainment; and no such reason existing, it is more difficult to discern the propriety of investing our governments with these superfluous and pernicious powers, by inference and construction.[73]

The overall trend was clear enough:

Under a reconciliation between republican and despotick principles, effected by the new idea of "sovereign servants," our legislatures are converted into British parliaments, daily new-modeling the substance of our government, by bodies politick, exclusive privileges, pensions, bounties, and judicial acts, comprising an arbitrary power of dispensing wealth or poverty to individuals and combinations at their pleasure.... If our system of government

---

73   *Ibid.*, 12.

produces these bitter fruits naturally, it is substantially European; and the world, after having contemplated with intense interest and eager solicitude the experiment of the United States, will be surprised to find, *that no experiment at all has been made*, and that it still remains to be discovered, whether a political system preferable to the British be within the scope of human capacity.[74]

Even Article I, Section 8, 18 — the "Sweeping Clause" ("To make all laws which shall be necessary and proper for carrying into execution the foregoing powers, and all other powers vested by this Constitution in the Government of the United States, or in any department or officer thereof") was not a general grant of unknown powers, even if Marshall found in the words "necessary and proper" license for innumerable convenient *means* yielding, in practice, un-enumerated powers.[75] In time, of course, all branches of the general government would share in Marshall's captured loot.

Spherical Sovereignty vs. Division and Limitation of Powers

McCulloch v. Maryland (1819) made much of the supremacy, superiority, etc. of Congress in its *sphere* of action. Taylor noted that "'sphere' conveys an idea of something limited, in which sense it is correctly applied to our governments by the Federalist... but I confess myself extremely puzzled to discern, how this word... can be converted into a substantive uncircumscribed, by the help of the adjective 'sovereign.'" He continues: "If the sovereignty of the spheres means any sovereignty at all, it supersedes the sovereignty of the people..."[76]

---

74   *Ibid.*, preface, 1-2 (emphasis supplied).

75   See Gerald Gunther, ed., *John Marshall's Defense of McCulloch v. Maryland* (Stanford, CA: Stanford University Press, 1969), for the essays by Spencer Roane and "Amphicyton" attacking the decision.

76   Taylor, *Construction Construed*, 99-100.

Taylor is not objecting to spheres, but to *sovereignty* in them. He quotes Dr. David Ramsay of South Carolina, the first historian of the American Revolution: "The rejection of British *sovereignty* therefore drew after it the necessity of fixing on some *other principle* of government."[77] For Taylor, this alternate principle rested on actual delegation by real principals to real (and mere) *agents*. Accordingly, *no one* had any "inherent" powers on any basis. Further: "There is no phrase in the constitution which even insinuates that the actual divisions of power should be altered or impaired by incidental or implied powers." It was true, he conceded, that "Individual spheres or departments are easily persuaded, like Kings, that a subordination to themselves would be better for a nation, than the occasional collisions produced by a division and limitation of power." Here was the danger: "A jurisdiction, limited by its own will, is an unlimited jurisdiction."[78]

Taylor preferred "occasional collisions" between concurrent jurisdictions to claims of supremacy or sovereignty. Instead of making Congress, an executive, or a court supreme in its sphere, our system was "founded in the principle of co-ordinate political departments, intended as *checks upon each other*, only invested with defined and limited powers, and subjected to the sovereignty, supremacy, and paramount power, superintendance and controul *of the people...*"[79] The Court's invention of "spherical sovereignty" actually overthrew the proper distribution of powers: "A supreme power able to abolish collisions, is also able to abolish checks, and there can be no checks without collisions." In America, we "have preferred checks and collisions, to a *dictatorship of one department*, under the supremacy of the people...."[80] Instead, under "the concurrent power of taxation," Congress and the states "may each pass a law, both of which may be constitutional, and

---

77 *Ibid.*, 63.

78 *Ibid.*, 109, 116, 131.

79 *Ibid.*, 139 (emphasis supplied).

80 *Ibid.*, 169-170 (emphasis supplied).

yet these laws may clash with, or impede each other.... For this clashing the constitution makes no provision."[81]

Taylor thought that the Court was claiming a kind of royal prerogative for Congress, including the power to "remove all obstacles to its action." Marshall sought "to unite an extension of power with an apparent adherence to the words of the constitution." The country not being "ripe" for the full doctrine of inherent sovereignty, "it was necessary to hook every implied, to some delegated power...."[82] This is still the practice of a continental state which shelters a massive regulatory state under the shed roof of the commerce clause and houses a worldwide military empire under the shabby lean-to of "defense."

On Taylor's argument, powers, where they exist, were *delegated* by actual Americans, and not by a dozen or so 18th-century paragraphs drifting heavenward while "mediating" some kind of Hegelian sovereignty to the three departments.[83] What is delegated, ought to be subject to recall. Taylor's view thus differs greatly from currently trendy but highly artificial and structuralist notions of the separation of powers deployed, for example, by "conservative" unitary executive theorists associated with the George W. Bush administration's lately famous "torture memos."[84]

Taylor v. Marshall and Sutherland

Partisans of central power can rely on John Marshall's assaults on limited and enumerated powers. They can likewise rely on Justice George Sutherland's dicta in *United States v. Curtiss-Wright* (1936) for the "inherency" of unnamed presidential powers. Sutherland asserted that George the Third's sovereign

---

81   *Ibid.*, 173.

82   *Ibid.*, 161-162, 178.

83   The usually reliable legal historian Edward S. Corwin resorts to the rather Hegelian term "mediate" on his way to stuffing the Curtiss-Wright decision (1936), somehow, into the constitution. *The President: Office and Powers* (New York: New York University Press, 1957), 172.

84   Taylor noted that federal powers were "frequently marked" in the federal Constitution, while those of the states were "left chiefly unlimited (*Construction Construed*, 109).

prerogative powers over foreign affairs and war had lighted upon the American executive, as soon as that wonderful appliance was on hand.[85] But Taylor saw through such arguments before they were made:

> The rights of declaring war, and of creating corporations or granting exclusive privileges, as considered by the writers upon the laws of nations, were rights of sovereignty; but the case of war is specially provided for by the federal constitution, because the federal government, as having no sovereignty, could not other wise have declared it... As the powers of making war and peace were necessary, it became necessary also to provide for them, not as emanations from the principle of a sovereignty in governments, but as delegated powers conferred by the social sovereignty, or natural right of self-government... No powers in relation to war are derived from the old doctrine of a sovereignty in governments under our system; and none can be justly inferred from the conclusions of the writers upon the laws of nations, deduced from that old doctrine. [86]

Taylor makes the interesting observation that the Court sought to "overthrow" such homegrown American reasoning "by inferring the powers of sovereignty from a delegated power; as the power of establishing banks, from the power of taxation..." Those who reasoned from delegated powers to a general (federal) sovereignty, as understood by international lawyers, erred in several particulars:

---

85   *United States v. Curtiss-Wright Export Corporation* (1936). See Michael D. Ramsey, "Why Curtiss-Wright Is Wrong: The Myth of Extraconstitutional Foreign Affairs Power," *William & Mary Law Review*, 42 (December 2000), 1-47, at http://papers.ssrn.com/papers. taf?abstract_id=223759). On Sutherland's use of framer James Wilson, see Walter H. Bennett, "Twentieth-Century Theories of the Nature of the Union," *Journal of Politics*, 8 (May 1946), 165-166.

86   Taylor, *Construction Construed*, 280 (emphasis supplied).

When two nations are at war, a third may subject itself to a legitimate attack from either, by certain actions; yet even in this case, which calls for *a prompt decision*, the constitution pays no regard to the idea of a spherical sovereignty; and disregarding the language of the laws of nations, assigns the power, as in every other case where a declaration of war may be necessary, to a department, not as being sovereign, but as being a trustee of the sovereign power. This trustee alone possesses a right to involve the United States in war; and no other department, *nor any individual*, has a better right to do so, than *a constable* has to bring the same calamity upon England. As the laws of nations cannot deprive congress of any power with which it is invested by the constitution, so they cannot invest congress or any other department, with any power not bestowed by the constitution. If the laws of nations could bestow any powers under our system, there would be great difficulty in ascertaining the department which should receive them. They [those laws] contemplate the powers of declaring war and making peace, as residing in an *executive* department; but the constitution divides them, and *does not intrust the president* with either.[87]

The central question for Taylor was "whether *these laws of nations or our constitutions* have delegated powers to our political departments." If the former, the game was up and power would not and could not be limited; if the latter, "sovereignty and the laws of nations united cannot create corporations, nor confer any power whatsoever...[88]

---

87   *Ibid.*, 281 (emphasis supplied). The paragraph also shows that Taylor was not buying any "inherent" presidential war powers.

88   *Ibid.*, 282 (emphasis supplied).

The Pretended Security Supplied by Election

For Taylor, security against abuses of power does not arise from mere representation, or from election of the personnel of political departments; for if those can destroy the checks put upon them, then "mankind after a long travail have returned to the very doctrine they have been trying to abolish, namely, that they must inevitably elect between a despotism in one, a few, or in many, because representation may be trusted with unlimited power."[89] No one — a hereditary prince, an aristocracy, or elected officers — was to be trusted with such power. Taylor could not be caught in the swindle by which the friends of power bring forward the *empty marker* of "popular sovereignty,"[90] whenever real questions of self-government, states rights, or liberty intrude upon the normal operations of the state.

These issues were central for Taylor because of the *probable failure* of American republicanism if it adopted European (royalist) sovereignty as its legal basis. Listing some objections to such a legal foundation, he writes:

> 2. That a sovereign power over labour or property is less oppressive in the hands of an absolute monarch, than in those of a representative legislature. 3. That the error of trusting republican governments with this tyrannical power, has probably caused their premature deaths, because they are most likely to push it to excess.[91]

Thus, when Taylor pointed out the danger of "monarchism" — which he accused his opponents of favoring — he was not concerned solely with the executive or its corrupting influence,

---

89   *Ibid.*, 287.

90   On this, see Joshua Miller, "The Ghostly Body Politic: The Federalist Papers and Popular Sovereignty," *Political Theory*, 16 (February 1988), 99-119.

91   *Taylor, Construction Construed*, 341. On the possibility that sovereign republics or democracies will be more expensive and oppressive than monarchies, see Murray N. Rothbard, *Man, Economy and State*, II (Los Angeles: Nash Publishing, 1970 [1962], 828-829, and Hans-Hermann Hoppe, *Democracy, the God That Failed* (New Brunswick, NJ: Transaction Publishers, 2001).

nor was he engaged in name calling; instead, he was addressing the whole theoretical basis of their system. Sovereignty — taken as anything more than another word for self-government — would doom any republicanism worthy of the name.

New Views of the Constitution

New Views of the Constitution of the United States (1823) was Taylor's final statement on these matters. It was — for Taylor — unaccountably clear in style and presentation. In preparing it, he was able to use the recently published "journal" of the Constitutional Convention — that is, the minutes kept, as opposed to James Madison's famous and lengthy private journal, only published in 1840 — as well as the notes taken by Robert Yates of New York.[92]

Over the years, Taylor had avoided any notion of absolute sovereignty. To the extent that he used the word, he equated it with the fact of self-government. Naturally, this raises the question, who are the self-governing people? On this, Taylor became clearer as he went, coming to rest conceptually at the separate peoples of the several states. Any other conclusion conflicted with the outstanding historical facts. In *New Views*, he seeks to prove textually that the union was a "*union of states,* and not a union of individual men." There had been no single American people — no "fabulous consolidated American nation" and therefore nothing sustained the old consolidationist dodge of pretending the word "states" referred to state *governments* and *not* to state peoples.[93]

There is much of interest in *New Views*, but only a few key points will be noted here. Taylor finds ample ideological continuity between the Philadelphia conclave and later political tendencies. Taylor sees three forces at work in the convention: 1) monarchists

---

92   For Yates's journal, see Charles Callan Tansill, ed., *Documents Illustrative of the Formation of the Union of the American States* (Washington, DC: Government Printing Office, 1927), 746-843. James McClellan writes: "Madison's decision to withhold his convention notes may have seriously undermined the states' rights movement, or possibly doomed it." "Introduction" to John Taylor of Caroline, *New Views*, liii.

93   Taylor, *New Views*, 276 (emphasis supplied), 283-284.

led by Hamilton, 2) pragmatic, big-state centralizers led by Madison, and 3) federal republicans, including Luther Martin and Robert Yates. (The role of continental creditors in the centralizing parties is duly noticed.) The *Federalist Papers* "resumed" nationalist ideas expressed at Philadelphia and, therefore, amounted to a misleading, Swiftian "codicil" to the actual constitution. Self-named Federalists had sown much confusion. Between outright monarchism and federal republicanism (Taylor's creed) stood "Mr. Madison's didactick federalism" — a "hopeless idea of reconciling contradictions." This ideology now held the high ground of American thought and perpetuated Madison's "disagreements with himself." Here was the famous dual federalism discovered by a "mystical mode of construction." Here, too, were three alleged sources for a (final) national sovereignty "deposited" in two places — Congress (Hamilton) or the Supreme Court (Madison).[94]

Taylor gives a very astute analysis of Federalist ideology in relation both to Hamilton's English view of sovereignty[95] and Madison's self-inflicted contradictions. He laid out what Federalists had to assume in order to achieve their constructive results[96] and tested those assumptions against historical fact and everyday logic to produce an alternate reading of the constitution. As for the future, that was problematic. America's "money-hunting parties" were not fit guardians of state rights and would soon "be reduced to two, the geographical ins and outs of a concentrated supremacy." Full national sovereignty, once achieved, would merely produce Eastern, Southern, and Western geographical political blocs keen to control the federal apparatus out of mainly economic motives.[97]

---

94   *Ibid.*, 49, 356, 203, 378, 72 – 73, 268, 135, 191, 143.

95   *Ibid.*, 94.

96   In particular, they assumed (and had to) that their constitutional coup of 1787-1789 had established an effectively unitary state on the ruins of the Confederation. Thereafter, the task was simply one of using English legal precedents to manage thirteen or more large counties.

97   *Ibid.*, 309, 352, 322.

Part III.

The Political Economy of
John Taylor of Caroline

Republicanism and Liberalism Revisited

AS NOTED PREVIOUSLY, 18th-century Anglo-American opposition writers employed several political languages. One of these,
classical republicanism, asserted reciprocal causal relations between power and property such that a republic secures stability
and liberty by way of a "mixed constitution" resting on a broad
class of independent proprietors. Critics of England's post-1688
Whig Oligarchy and its state-financial revolution often deployed
this language. This allows many historians to read such "republicans" as vaguely outlined "agrarians" futilely resisting inevitable
capitalist development and *social change*.[98]

In the American context, as Taylor argued over and over again,
the archaic-republican theme of social "balance" between constitutionally embedded orders was thoroughly misleading. Even the
republican notions of "corruption" and "virtue" had somewhat
different meanings. As Robert Kelley writes, for Jeffersonians:

> ... the great danger for the public lay in the fact that
> aristocracies had more subtle weapons than their
> opponents. With their wealth they could buy off

---

98   "Social change" is the specter historians routinely invoke when they can't, or don't wish
to, explain what happened, or who did what to whom.

the opposition, could indeed recruit them. This was what made "corruption" perhaps the most resonant of all issues...[99]

And as Lance Banning notes, "The target was not business enterprise, not wealth itself, but a particular variety of paper wealth that seemed too closely tied to governmental favor."[100] A tour of Taylor's *Inquiry into the Principles and Policy of the Government of the United States*, finished in 1811 and published in 1814, will uncover many such themes.

Taylor's Political Economy as Revealed in the *Inquiry*

Owing to its long gestation, the *Inquiry* is a great handbook of republican ideas as understood in late 18th and early 19th-century Virginia. Taylor's "republicanism" was consistent and radical, but not especially anti-commercial, nor overly concerned with "virtue," and certainly not Rousseauian[101] or communitarian in any proto-socialist way. A rather wide-roaming answer to John Adams' *Defense of the American Constitutions,* the *Inquiry* covers the whole range of 17th and 18th-century political thought, English and continental alike, a great deal of English legal and political history, and much else besides.

A preliminary observation is that for Taylor, the political "common good" involves the maintaining of a liberal political order over time.[102] Part I of the *Inquiry* — "Aristocracy" — begins with a refutation of Adams' archaic-republican "numerical analysis" of

---

99   Robert Kelley, *The Transatlantic Persuasion: The Liberal-Democratic Mind in the Age of Gladstone* (New York: Alfred A. Knopf, 1969), 138. Cf. Emma Rothschild, *Economic Sentiments: Adam Smith, Condorcet, and the Enlightenment* (Cambridge, MA: Harvard University Press, 2001), 154.

100   Banning, 205.

101   A "revisionist" view of Rousseau would (if sustained) bring Taylor and Rousseau closer together. See Bertrand de Jouvenel, "Rousseau's Theory of the Forms of Government," in Maurice Cranston and Richard S. Peters, eds., *Hobbes and Rousseau* (Garden City, NY: Anchor Books, 1972), 484-497, and Giovanni Sartori, "Liberty and Law," in Kenneth S. Templeton, ed., *The Politicization of Society* (Indianapolis: Liberty Press, 1979), 274-289.

102   To this extent, Taylor's outlook has something in common with that of modern "liberal Aristotelians" influenced (one suspects mostly for the worse) by Ayn Rand.

states into government by one (monarchy), the few (aristocracy), and the many (democracy). In Taylor's view, Adams had failed to justify (practically) ancient Greek aristocracy. Further, Adams consistently overlooked the artificial causes of aristocratic wealth. Since the age of aristocracies, says Taylor, "knowledge and commerce" have eroded those orders.[103]

To answer Adams's archaic republicanism, Taylor, like many thinkers of his time, organized history into three ages, each with a corresponding artificial aristocracy: first, an age of superstition, then, a feudal age of conquest, and third, an age of paper and patronage. The last age was a present reality in Britain,[104] and the Federalist Party longed to have the British system here.

"Talent and virtue are now so widely distributed," writes Taylor, that such systems were unnecessary. As a result, "Modern taxes and frauds to collect money, and not ancient authors, will therefore afford the best evidence of its present character." Despite the irrelevance of the two earlier forms of aristocracy, Taylor as a thorough comparative anatomist examines them[105] before turning to artificial capital and credit as the probable sources of an American unnatural aristocracy.

Taylor observes that paper credit fled the field in the American Revolution and "anticipation"[106] proved delusive. Even so, paper systems won friends because paper stock is more profitable than slavery. Worse, we are exhorted to pay such public debts in the name of protecting property in general. It would be more honest for the stockjobbers to say: "Our purpose is to settle wealth and power upon a minority. It will be accomplished by national debt, paper corporations, and offices, civil and military."[107]

---

103   Taylor, *Inquiry*, 37-38, 42, 45.

104   Taylor, *Inquiry*, 54.

105   *Ibid.*, 57, 61.

106   By "anticipation" Taylor means the attempt to live on credit while passing along the costs to future generations. See *Inquiry*, 232. Anticipation "had fled disgracefully from the contest" (237).

107   Taylor, *Inquiry*, 63-66.

Though a nation may be enslaved by force (armies), or fraud (paper money), "few are jealous of stockjobbers." But paper stock is not a source of national strength; nor does wider access to monopoly cure its evils. A majority cannot live off a minority.[108] Taylor thought it strange that Americans had more readily spotted abuses of the taxing power under British rule, than under their own republic — especially since the upkeep of a paper aristocracy required higher taxes than a landed one did. As for the supposed English "balance" between orders, contended for by Adams, that social structure was long since overturned, hence the irrelevance of Shaftesbury's ideas on the matter.[109]

As to more modern forms of artificial property, Taylor writes that Americans had managed to "explode... the antiquated social compact dogma" only to submit to "the modern law charter dogma," which made new state-created rights and properties eternally inviolable. Such *English* "private property" did not suit America, despite the attempt under slogans about "publick faith" or "national credit" to make it a key moral precept, so as to sustain privilege.[110]

In Part 2, "The English vs. the American Policy," Taylor noted that Americans mean to *divide* power rather than "balance" it. Just as "'An uncertainty of law' is a 'glorious' object to avaricious lawyers," so, too, would "'An uncertainty of republicanism'... be an object, not less desirable to ambitious politicians."[111] To achieve his purpose of telling good governments from bad, Taylor adopted a classical liberal welfare analysis, which he built into his republican outlook. On this analysis, we see how false property must ally itself to justly acquired property while raising the cry of "Leveling" against critics of the former. Taylor writes: "I consider those possessions as property, which are fairly gained by talents

---

108   *Ibid.*, 67-71. "General incorporation" laws from the 1840s onward broadened access to monopoly privileges without removing their monopolistic character.

109   *Ibid.*, 73-74, 79, 108.

110   *Ibid.*, 85, 87, 89. See, for example, *Fletcher v. Peck* (1810), in which Justice John Marshall, speaking for the Supreme Court, invoked the federal constitution's contract clause (Article I, Section 10) to save the Yazoo land boodlers and their subsequent buyers.

111   *Ibid.*, 104, 118.

and industry, or are capable of subsisting, without taking property from others by law." On such a view, proto-socialist leveling and aristocratic-feudal exactions had much in common. For just this reason, "balanced orders" were hardly needed to shield us from phantom leveling, which "never will have advocates" in North America.[112]

Taking a Protestant and liberal historical line, Taylor writes that printing lessened ignorance and "commerce and alienation gradually destroyed the balance of property and power among orders." With the old order worn away, "taxation becomes the only engine for distributing and balancing property; and must arrange society into the two orders of payers and receivers."[113] Given that "human nature is compounded of good and evil qualities," writes Taylor, "government ought to be modeled with a view to the preservation of the good and the control of the evil." In his view, "political law" (constitutions) will keep governments moral. Even so, governments may be "vicious" owing to bad incentives.[114] Constitutions may be improved.

In Part 3, "The Evils of the US Government," Taylor focused on constitutional defects, and urged amendments. The American executive was so constructed as "to excite evil moral qualities" and drive us "toward force and fraud." Elections alone could not correct the evil.[115] Secrecy and exploitation of war powers might allow a president, who already had more effective power than Caesar needed to enslave Rome, to overawe the people. Exclusive control of military patronage, and its extension during war, inclined the president to war, while "the military power is not even divided, and is only subjected in a state of complete accumulation, to the suffrages of an unarmed people."[116] Hence, Taylor's commitment

---

112   Ibid., 118, 124, 127-128. Cf. Percy Bysshe Shelley, *Political Writings*, ed. Roland A. Duerksen (New York: Meredith Corporation, 1970), 138-143, on the two kinds of property.

113   Taylor, *Inquiry*, 131, 135. John C. Calhoun made the same point in his *Disquisition*; the relevant passages are quoted in Murray N. Rothbard, *Power and Market* (Menlo Park, CA: Institute for Humane Studies, 1970), 12-13.

114   Taylor, *Inquiry*, 150, 161-163.

115   Ibid., 169, 171.

116   Ibid., 172-174, 177.

to a genuine revitalized militia system — for practical, political (and even liberal) reasons — and not out of ancient republican theory. The treaty and appointment powers added to the president's weaponry, and to his already excessive military power was "subjoined a mass of civil power" and "the prerogative of conferring lucrative offices upon members of congress," which allowed the president to control the legislature. Election "procures a confidence [for the president] which has no foundation." By contrast, the states had made much headway in "unmonarchising" the executive by various devices.[117]

Anticipating Lord Acton, Taylor writes that, "Power changes moral character, and private life regenerates it" — a republican enough sentiment in Virginia, but not perhaps in ancient Greece. Absent English social orders, "the only reason for a strong executive, does not exist..." Closing his remarks on the presidency, Taylor can find no "reason why war, peace, appointments to office, or the dispensation of publick money, should have been counted in the catalogue of the [executive], except for the efficacy of these powers in one man for begetting tyranny...."[118]

Turning to the federal courts, the danger there lies in their ability to convert their "independence" from other political branches into "an immoveable power of construction" *over* the constitution and thus over other branches, and finally, over the sovereignty of the people. This outcome looms if judges successfully assert "the exclusive right of declaring a law void."[119]

In Part 4, "Funding," Taylor deconstructs national (or public) debt, which arises from a particular generation's wish "to *antici-pate* the riches of posterity and bequeath it their misfortunes."[120] He writes:

---

117   *Ibid.*, 178-179, 181, 183, 185.

118   *Ibid.*, 187-188, 195.

119   *Ibid.*, 195-200, 200-215.

120   *Ibid.*, 232, emphasis supplied.

But an opinion that it is possible, for the present generation to seize and use the property of future generations, has produced to both the parties concerned, effects of the same complexion with the usual fruits of national errour. The present age is cajoled to tax and enslave itself by the errour of believing that it taxes and enslaves future ages to enrich itself; and the future ages submit to taxation and slavery, by being reduced into an erroneous opinion, that the present age have a right to inflict upon them these calamities.[121]

Taylor again remarks how "anticipation" fled the field in the Revolution after distracting Americans from the real means of winning the war: a public spirit able to overcome the usual "free rider" problems.[122] In addition, a false analogy with everyday commercial borrowing at interest muddled the paper stock/public debt question. Paper stock/national debt is not necessary in order for commerce to flourish, even if, coincidentally, "they exist together in England. That one is the bane of the other, we have already inferred from the necessity of England to resort to war and conquest to cultivate her commerce." Paper contrivances are mere "signs or representations" of real things, and paper stock is in fact a kind of tax on money and its circulation.[123]

At the end of the *Inquiry*, Taylor comes back once more to Americans' earlier experience of paper money, arguing that "the final success of the revolutionary war, was produced *by the depreciation* of the paper money, and the other causes by which government was prevented from creating parties of interest by pecuniary laws; an impotence which guaranteed the patriotism

---

121   *Ibid.*, 233.

122   Successful revolution involves collective action motivated by shared ideas, and an exact "fairness" to participant individuals does not enter into it. See Jeffrey Rogers Hummel, "The Will to Be Free: The Role of Ideology in National Defense," *Independent Review*, 5 (Spring 2001), 523-537.

123   Taylor, *Inquiry*, 236-237, 239-240, 249-251.

even of both ins and outs."[124] Mark well that Taylor does not equate the success of the Revolution with the success of *the government*. He is happy that the Revolution "succeeded" *without* — indeed because governments could not create — permanent public debt in lieu of paper currency.[125]

Extending his dialectic of true and false property, Taylor observes: "Despotick power strives to blend itself with a legitimate government, as paper stock does with private property..."[126] This was the rule in England, even if new players now ran the game:

> The nobility in England no longer foment wars, because they are not aggrandized by it, and war has been still more ardently fomented in that country than ever, because their system of paper and patronage gain spoil by it in any event. Conquest furnishes it with funds on which to bottom more stock, and the war which made the conquest, with a pretext for quartering more patronage and paper in its own nation. Is not that a separate aristocratical interest which gains more by war and conquest, than orders of titled nobility formerly did?

Increased taxes were another consequence of such systems.[127]

In Part 5, "Banking," Taylor characterizes banking as generally bad as currently practiced. He notes the advantage of coin in being difficult to multiply, that is, inflate. He sees bank profits as a "tax"

---

124   *Ibid.*, 555 (emphasis supplied); and see E. James Ferguson, *The Power of the Purse* (Chapel Hill, NC: University of North Carolina Press, 1961).

125   Here, Taylor is supported by the Austrian economist and historian Murray N. Rothbard: "the cheap money and price control policies burdened rather than fostered the revolutionary effort" (*Conceived in Liberty*, IV [New Rochelle, NY: Arlington House, 1979], 379, and ff.), and factually by Ferguson, *Power of the Purse*.

126   Taylor, *Inquiry*, 258.

127   *Ibid.*, 261-263 (emphasis supplied, 261).

paid by the public to privileged corporations.[128] The Bank of the United States is of course bad, although Taylor thinks that the old Bank of Pennsylvania can be defended.[129]

Taylor compares patronage gained by banking with that obtained by conquest. He writes that if patronage "is obtained by foreign conquest, as in the acquisition of India by England, the people still suffer *by the unconstitutional power* it confers," even if patronage "is infinitely more calamitous to a nation, when gotten by domestick operations."[130] The phrase which I have italicized is surely one of the earlier notices of the problem of "blowback" in Anglo-American writing! (Alas, that financial-industrial game could not go on successfully forever. Writing specifically of the British Empire in India, historian David Washbrook notes that "reliance on external agencies came to have its costs. British capitalism tended to become parasitic: living off the easy profits of imperialism affected the character of its later drives towards 'rationalization' and corporatism."[131])

Taylor also spots the very monetary illusion that would one day become a centerpiece of Keynesian economic policy: "an advancement of the price of labour, pari passu, would produce neither gain nor loss." He shows a good grasp of international money and goods flows, whether of paper, specie, or commodities. He again compares bank slavery to chattel slavery.[132] Taylor also notices than under hard money, any supply of money is optimal[133] and discusses the bankers' "privilege" of operating on fractional reserves. With increased interest (subsequently counted as assets) and multiple lending of the same capital (as if it were really on hand, warehoused), massive transfers of *real goods* proceed under

---

128 *Ibid.*, 267, 269, 273.

129 *Ibid.*, 275-276, 279-280. As an empirical matter, the Bank of the U.S. did have corrupt directors: see Sean Wilentz, *The Rise of American Democracy: Jefferson to Lincoln* (New York: W. W. Norton, 2005), 214-216 and 843-844, notes.

130 Taylor, *Inquiry*, 287 (emphasis supplied).

131 David Washbrook, "South Asia, the World System, and World Capitalism," *Journal of Asian Studies*, 49 (August 1990), 502.

132 *Taylor, Inquiry*, 306-310, 313, 317.

133 *Ibid.*, 319. Cf. Rothbard, *Man, Economy and State,* II, 669-671.

a monetary illusion. Monetary fluctuations accompany the process. Taylor comments, "The tyranny of fraud is not less oppressive than that of force."[134] Despite all the theoretical knowledge and historical experience that could be brought to bear on these questions, writes Taylor, Americans have allowed the experiments of Walpole to be repeated on our soil.[135]

In Part 6, "The Good Moral Principles of the US Govt.," Taylor proceeds (he says) on the ground of the laws of nature. These require political equality. (All this is part of Taylor's polemic against John Adams' fixed social orders.) Taylor wants to see real divisions of power and real agency. He asserts that popular sovereignty "flows out of each man's right to govern himself."[136]

Taylor comments that, "Oaths of agents are prescribed to enforce, not to destroy, the duties of agency"[137] — a rather different view than that of Lincoln and other defenders of presidential prerogative, who take the oath as *another source* of power. He repeats that self-government is superior to sovereignty. A rather vague discussion of the sovereignty of the people follows. He observes that no *governments* — federal or state — could, as subordinate agents, dissolve the union on their own motion. Taylor hails election, divisions of power, and an armed people as the means to secure republican liberty.[138]

Again, sounding like Lord Acton, Taylor asserts that "Great power often corrupts virtue; it invariably renders vice more malignant... In proportion as the powers of governments increase, both its own character and that of the people becomes worse." As for what we now call National Security, "A protector is unexceptionally a master... without a 'well-regulated militia,' the military sovereignty of a nation, exactly resembles its civil society

---

134   Taylor, *Inquiry*, 331-332, 341, 346. Jesús Huerta de Soto's *Money, Bank Credit, and Economic Cycles* (Auburn AL: Ludwig von Mises Institute, 2006) sustains (and goes beyond) Taylor's views on money and banking.

135   Taylor, *Inquiry*, 347.

136   *Ibid.*, 357-358, 364-365.

137   *Ibid.*, 370.

138   *Ibid.*, 378-379.

under a government of hereditary orders."[139] Addressing the Alien and Sedition Acts, Taylor urges that freedom of discussion arises directly from the right of self-government, while the election of mere agents is *not* a participation in the sovereignty. The sovereignty created the "political law" which uses elections as one device for dividing and controlling power.[140] Contrary to Adams and others, the procedure for amending the constitution and the makeup of the US Senate do not at all answer to English-style orders.[141]

In Part 7, "Authority," Taylor notes the perils of confidence. He deploys the words of the revolutionary John Adams against the later John Adams. He undertakes further repudiations of "virtue" as the basis of republicanism:

> If virtue, *as a basis of government*, be understood to mean, not that the principles of the government, but that the individuals composing the nation must be virtuous, then republicks would be found in the self same principle with monarchies, namely, the evanescent qualities of individuals. But interest is a better and more permanent basis... Its wonderful capacity for concretion bestows on noble orders, hierarchies and stockjobbers, power for oppression, and loyalty to each other in defrauding; and why may it not also secure the fidelity of nations to themselves, though composed of people equally as vicious?[142]

---

139   *Ibid.*, 383, 396.

140   *Ibid.*, 422, discussion of Sedition Laws, 425-437.

141   *Ibid.*, 437-444.

142   *Ibid.*, 447, 452-458, quotation at 461 (emphasis supplied). Here Taylor's ideas call to mind modern public choice theory — with the reservation that Taylor's analyses often seem superior. Perhaps these moderns should be called "neo-Taylorites."

Taylor reviews Adams's ideas in relation to the debate between Malthus and Godwin.[143] He shows himself to be more impressed with Godwin, and displays much interest in the plight of the working poor in England. Along the way, referring to English politics after the Glorious Revolution, he aims at an inviting target:

> The English writers during the specified period, contain whatever is to be found in the Federalist; but all their theories sunk, as soon as they were promulgated; in a vortex of corruption... What is to keep the same doctrines from the same fate, or shield the United States under their guidance, from the same effects?[144]

In Part 8, "The Mode of Infusing Aristocracy into the United States," Taylor avers that, "Aristocracy is no where agrarian." He notes that a paper-military-patronage aristocracy gets along without titles, but is no less dangerous for that. (Today, we might say military-industrial-financial-congressional-university complex.) "Money and armies are the instruments of power," writes Taylor, in another post-Harringtonian statement.[145] Such are the main lines of attack in Taylor's *Inquiry*, lines continued in *Tyranny Unmasked*.

Tyranny Unmasked, written (as noted above) in response to Congressional support for protective tariffs, carried forward Taylor's politically grounded class analysis. Along with the usual fireworks, the book displays great sociological penetration. One example will suffice here. Summing up the consequences and character of the combined stock-jobbing and tariff system, Taylor declares it "incapable of contradiction" that,

---

143   *Ibid.*, 466-473. For discussion of the Malthus-Godwin debate paralleling Taylor's, see Murray N. Rothbard, *Economic Thought Before Adam Smith* (Vol. I of *An Austrian Perspective on the History of Economic Thought*, Cheltenham, UK: Edward Elgar, 1995), 481-492.

144   Taylor, *Inquiry*, 467.

145   *Ibid.*, 477-479.

... no species of property-transferring policy, past or existing, foreign or domestick, ever did or ever can enrich the labouring classes of any society whatever; but that it universally impoverishes them.... The mercantile class, as merchants only, must be impoverished by this policy; but a few individuals of this class, more frequently evade its oppression, than of other labouring classes, by blending the capitalist with the mercantile character; and becoming bankers, lenders to government, or factory owners. So far also, as the agricultural and mechanical classes, are interspersed with individuals endowed with pecuniary privileges, such individuals derive emolument from the property-transferring policy, not as mechanicks or agriculturists, but in their privileged characters. Those who gain more by banking, by the protecting-duty monopoly, or by loaning money to the government, than they lose by these property-transferring machines, constitute no exception to the fact, that the property-transferring policy invariably impoverishes all labouring and productive classes. A few individuals are enriched by every species of tyranny, as its essence in civilized countries consists of transferring property by laws.[146]

Here, methodological individualism meets class conflict kindled by the property-transferring activities of the state, and the resulting discussion does not so much "foretell" Marx's style of analysis as demonstrate a similar but earlier analysis.

---

146   Taylor, *Tyranny Unmasked*, 267.

Liberal Class Analysis: Labor, State, and Markets

Taylor seems to have been perfectly sincere when he championed "labour" and "agriculture" and denounced paper feudalists. It would be unhistorical to take him as seizing on the word "labour" in the service of hypocrisy. In truth, Taylor was applying a class-conflict analysis that contrasted property created by political force and fraud with property earned through productive effort (whether by farmers, entrepreneurs, tradesmen, or laborers). At a time when special interests, classes, and even whole regions sought to batten on the state, such an analysis was an important moral and sociological tool.[147]

There is a striking resemblance between Taylor's sociology and that of the French Restoration liberal school of J.B. Say, Charles Comte, Charles Dunoyer, and Augustin Thierry. In their doctrine of *"industrialisme,"* we meet with the same distinction between true and false property and between productive and parasitic social classes understood in relation to state power. We also find the same readiness to reduce government's role to some strict minimum, the same ascription of class conflict to political measures.[148] Taylor also bears comparison with the English Ricardian socialists of the 1820s and 1830s ("socialists" because they converted David Ricardo's economics into an attack on English capitalism). In 1987, economist Michael Perelman characterized Taylor as the "most eloquent" of those who used the term "labor" for "the activities of almost everyone other than those who profited from extending credit," and added that "the similarity between the rhetoric of

---

147   E.P. Thompson refers to 18th-century England as a "banana republic," adding, "The Whigs, in the 1720s, were a curious junta of political speculators and speculative politicians, stock-jobbers, officers grown fat on Marlborough's wars, time-serving dependants in the law and the Church, and great landed magnates." *Whigs and Hunters: The Origins of the Black Act* (New York: Random House, 1975), 197-198.

148   On the "industrialist" school, see Leonard P. Liggio, "Charles Dunoyer and French Classical Liberalism," *Journal of Libertarian Studies*, I (Summer 1977), 153-178. Cf. Ralph Raico, "Classical Liberal Exploitation Theory: A Comment on Professor Liggio's Paper," *Ibid.*, 179-83, and "Liberalism, Marxism, and the State," *Cato Journal*, 11 (Winter 1992), 391-404.

Taylor, an archconservative, and the so-called Ricardian socialists would make an excellent subject for further study."[149]

Jefferson and Taylor were conversant with the English economists and with the French *laissez-faire* liberals Jean-Baptiste Say and Antoine Louis Claude Destutt de Tracy.[150] But Taylor has flashes of complete originality. After all, none (or very few) of the French or English writers undertook to apply their critical ideas to the new American system, since they fondly hoped it would repudiate European mercantilism entirely. Taylor was breaking new ground.

In fact, Taylor's critique is ideally fitted for grappling with the state-assisted triumph of the modern corporation, ending in a thoroughly rationalized corporatist order. Here it would be better to reexamine the legal form of the corporation itself, instead of blaming Taylor and Jefferson (as modern critics like Hofstadter were wont to do) for those late 19th-century corporate defenders who used their language. It was Taylor after all who wrote, "There are some words innately despotic" — notably "hierarchy" and "corporation." He added: "Both are appurtenances of sovereignty, and sovereignty being despotick because it is indefinite, both are appurtenances of despotism."[151] On this line, we might begin to see 19th-century general incorporation laws as a "democratic" broadening of access to special privileges that were illegitimate and *mala in se*.[152] Taylor already knew that giving monopolistic

---

149   See Thomas Hodgskin, *The Natural and Artificial Right of Property* (London: B. Steil, 1832) and Michael Perelman, *Marx's Crises Theory: Scarcity, Labor, and Finance* (New York: Praeger, 1987), 174-175 (and see the chapter "Fictitious Capital and the Crisis Theory").

150   Historian John F. Devanny, Jr. compares Taylor with Tracy in "Some Notes on Certain Proto-Austrian Features in the Economic Thought of John Taylor of Caroline," unpublished paper, Austrian Scholars Conference, March 31, 2001, 4. Jefferson oversaw the translation from French of Tracy's *Treatise on Political Economy*.

151   Taylor, *Construction Construed*, 87.

152   See James F. Becker, "The Corporation and Its Liberal Analysis," *Journal of the History of Ideas*, 30 (January-March 1969), 69-84; Frank van Dun, "Personal Freedom versus Corporate Liberties," *Philosophical Notes*, No. 76 (London: Libertarian Alliance, 2006), 1-19; James Cox, "On Unlimited Liability, Appendix G," in Condy Raguet, *A Treatise on Currency and Banking* (London: Ridgway, 1839), 260-288; and Piet-Hein Van Eeghen, "The Corporation at Issue, Part I: The Clash with Classical Liberal Values and the Negative Consequences for Capitalist Practice," *Journal of Libertarian Studies*, 19 (Summer 2005), 49-70, and "The Corporation at Issue, Part II," *JLS*, 19 (Fall 2005), 37-57. On the creation of a rationalized, corporatist order, see, out of a large literature: Gabriel Kolko, *The Triumph of*

privilege a wider base did not resolve the problem or fact of monopoly.[153] A search for the deeper roots of American corporatism might well demonstrate the relevance of Taylor's critique across all of American history.

In any case, Taylor saw great extremes of wealth and poverty as the invariable result of extra-economic coercion and deceit.[154] In his treatment of wealth and power, Taylor, the successful Southern planter, perhaps resembled no other Anglo-American *laissez faire* liberal as much as Thomas Paine, a self-taught petty bourgeois radical. With the obvious exception of slavery, which Paine denounced, and Taylor despaired of changing, the two men had much in common.[155]

Taylor does, indeed, sound puzzlingly proto-Marxist at times. This confuses commentators who imagine that any analysis involving class conflict and exploitation necessarily "looks forward" to Marxism. Compare Louis Hartz: "Taylor's historical theory is a kind of Marxism ending in a smashing anticlimax."[156] And here is Taylor answering the question of why protectionism has not helped English workingmen: "Because it has established a monopoly which operates only in favour of their employers, increases the expenses of government, and feeds unproductive capital by sacrificing productive labour." This is especially true, he writes, in agricultural and seafaring occupations, where the workers have "very little capital except their bodily labour." Here is "Marx's" category

---

Conservatism (Chicago: Quadrangle, 1967), William Appleman Williams, *The Contours of American History* (New York: New Viewpoints, 1973 [1961]), Part III, James Weinstein, *The Corporate Ideal in the Liberal State, 1900-1981* (Boston: Beacon Press, 1968), James Gilbert, *Designing the Industrial State: The Intellectual Pursuit of Collectivism in America, 1880-1940* (Chicago: Quadrangle Books, 1972), David F. Noble, *America by Design: Science, Technology, and the Rise of Corporate Capitalism* (New York: Oxford, 1977), and R. Jeffrey Lustig, *Corporate Liberalism: The Origins of Modern American Political Theory, 1890-1920* (Berkeley, CA: University of California Press, 1982).

153   Taylor, *Inquiry*, 67-71.

154   Beard, *Economic Origins*, 323-325.

155   On Paine, see Eric Foner, *Tom Paine and Revolutionary America* (New York: Oxford University Press, 1976), which brings out the radical liberal dimension of Paine's ideas.

156   Hartz, *Liberal Tradition in America*, 126.

of labor-power several decades before Marx.[157] (And who should grasp the value created by labor better than an owner of laborers?) But no, Taylor does not need to be a proto-Marxist. Radical classical liberals and English Ricardian socialists had their own analysis of political-economic structures founded on a state-centered theory of social conflict. This was a theory of plunder or spoliation, with the state and its legal system making important — and rather "autonomous" — contributions to artificial class differences and social conflict.[158]

Slavery and Colonization

Taylor's greatest "deviation" from political liberalism came (as with other Southern thinkers) over slavery. Here, like centralizing Whigs concerned with international relations, the planters could plead necessity (but with more justice). As often happens in human affairs, those philanthropists most open to the radical and simple solution, immediate emancipation, were those who would be least affected by such a revolution in social relations. It is a truism that the growth of antislavery feeling in the northern states drove Southern spokesmen to focus on their legal rights in the union and later to defend slavery in the abstract.

Taylor writes in *Arator*:

> The fact is, that negro slavery is an evil which the United States must look in the face. To whine over it, is cowardly; to aggravate it, criminal; and to forbear to alleviate it, because it cannot be wholly cured, foolish.[159]

---

157 Taylor, *Construction Construed*, 228-229. Cf. slavery apologist George Fitzhugh's labor theory of value, as discussed by Eugene D. Genovese, *The World the Slaveholders Made* (New York: Vintage Books, 1971), 174-184.

158 See Liggio, "Charles Dunoyer and French Classical Liberalism," and Raico, "Classical Liberal Exploitation Theory." Recall that "paper and patronage gain spoil" (*Inquiry*, 261, emphasis supplied).

159 Taylor, *Arator*, 180.

As a successful planter, Taylor was deeply involved in the use of slave labor; as a spokesman for Virginia, he could not escape certain dilemmas arising from that illiberal institution. Unlike Jefferson, whose evasions and contradictions fascinate historians, Taylor met slavery (nearly) head on. It was an evil, he said, but one without a short-term cure, what with the constant threat of slave revolt, racial struggle, and general slaughter. In time, he wrote,

> If England and America would erect and foster a settlement of free negroes in some fertile part of Africa, it would soon subsist by its own energies. Slavery might then be gradually re-exported, and philanthropy gratified by a slow reanimation of the virtue, religion and liberty of the negroes, instead of being again afflicted with the effects of her own rash attempts suddenly to change human nature.[160]

All through his writings, Taylor was quite realistic on the subject of slavery. Recall his assertions, already mentioned, that financial exploitation is even worse than chattel slavery, which implicitly concedes that chattel slavery was exploitative. He writes further:

> It has often been said, that poor labouring people in Europe, encounter more penury and distress than the Negro slaves in the United States. The profit *extorted* from the negro slave is moderated by the immediate interest of his master in his existence. It is moderated by the master's benevolence, and by his respect for his own reputation. But the slave of stock enjoys none of these ameliorations....[161]

---

160   *Ibid.*, 125, and see 119-125, 176-181, as well as Keith M. Bailor, "John Taylor of Caroline: Continuity, Change, and Discontinuity in Virginia's Sentiments toward Slavery, 1790-1820," *Virginia Magazine of History and Biography*, 75 (July 1967), 290-304.

161   Taylor, *Inquiry*, 317.

Finally, in rejecting claims that the existence of superior managerial intelligence in some people permitted establishment of privileged orders, Taylor notes the "evils resulting from the usurpations of a power of direction, founded in the false assumption of superior intelligence...." In fact, "freedom of intelligence" made church and state "more productive" of good for mankind and we would logically expect similar results in the case of "labour" (= all unprivileged productive activities). Taylor asks rhetorically:

> Are slaves free, because their labour is made more productive, (if such be the fact,) by the intelligence of their masters? Is the white population of the world justified in converting to its own use the labour of Africa, on account of superiority of intellect? Would the intelligence of the negroes in Africa be diminished by a freedom of labour?[162]

The whole discussion, carried over into the next page, assumes an answer of "no."

Unfortunately, actual circumstances left Taylor with no interim choice, if he sought one, except to defend slavery as it existed, especially after he saw how the Federalists and their heirs meant to employ the slavery issue to curtail Southern power in the Union. Taylor's espousal of eventual colonization of emancipated blacks "back" to Africa shows that he, like all white American statesmen of his day, intended America to be a white man's country. In this, Taylor was probably no worse than his contemporaries and successors, including Abraham Lincoln.[163]

---

162   Taylor, *Construction Construed*, 250.

163   On the limitations, North and South, of American thinking on slavery, see Robert McColley, *Slavery and Jeffersonian Virginia* (Chicago: University of Illinois Press, 1973), esp. 171, 185-186; Duncan J. MacLeod, *Slavery, Race and the American Revolution* (Cambridge: Harvard University Press, 1974), 89-94; and Donald Livingston, "A Moral Accounting of the Union and Confederacy," *Journal of Libertarian Studies*, 16 (Spring 2022), 57-101.

State-Financial Revolution and Paper Aristocracy

In words reminiscent of Harrington, Taylor writes that "enormous political power invariably accumulates enormous wealth, and enormous wealth invariably accumulates enormous political power."[164] It is possible that he viewed coercive political power as the primary causal element in this reciprocal relationship. Taylor's attack on "paper feudalism" asserted the parasitic character of state-created capital. At best, subsidized capital transferred real wealth to new owners from the economically productive; at worst, it cemented an aggressive alliance of artificial capitalists, corrupt courtiers, and officials.[165]

Further, increased taxation necessary to pay the expenses of the public debt drained additional real wealth away from productive uses. Public credit made possible the standing army, an instrument of constitutional subversion and imperialist war. England, Taylor continually noted, had followed this road to ruin and America was on the same path under Federalists and Republicans alike.[166]

And here, we are finally in a position to understand the actual meaning of Jefferson's constant references to the necessity of "periodic revolutions." Consistent with Taylor's views on state-created artificial orders, the people must somehow be able to undo these creations, even if the Supreme Court was hard at work turning them into sacred, permanent entitlements through English charter-law dogma. The Yazoo land grants come readily to mind. The legislature of Georgia handed out millions of acres of western land to those who corrupted and bribed them. When a later legislature

---

164   Taylor, *Tyranny Unmasked*, 194.

165   Cf. Karl Marx: "...public debt becomes one of the most powerful levers of primitive accumulation" (*Capital*, I [New York: International Publishers, 1967], 754-57). Marx cites Lord Bolingbroke's works as evidence for widespread opposition to government finance.

166   Compare a recent book on the current American debt crisis: Bill Bonner and Addison Wiggin, *Empire of Debt: The Rise of an Epic Financial Crisis* (Hoboken, NJ: John Wiley & Sons, 2006).

undid the grant, Chief Justice John Marshall found that the original act had become a sacred trust under the contract clause — a textbook example of why Taylor hated "charter law."[167]

---

167   Taylor, *Inquiry*, 546-547, against contract clause as read by the U.S. Supreme Court. See *Fletcher v. Peck* (1810), rescuing the Yazoo claimants. Cf. Michael Hudson, "A Cautionary Tale About Politicos and Financiers: Mr. Paulson and the New Yazoo Land Scandal," *Counterpunch*, September 23, 2008, at http://michael-hudson.com/articles/financial/080923PaulsonYazooLand.html .

Part IV.

War, Peace, and Empire

War Finance

DISILLUSIONED BY THE POLICIES of his Republican allies, who had leapt unprepared into the War of 1812, Taylor writes: "War is among the most plausible means used to delude a nation into the errour of anticipation," or living on credit:

> Yet it cannot bring up from futurity a gun, a soldier, a ration, or a cartridge. The present generation suffers every hardship and cost of war, although anticipation pretends that it is covered by future generations. And this delusion is used to involve nations in wars, which they would never commence, if they knew that all the expense would fall upon themselves. It is twice suffered; by the living, who supply all the expenses of war; by the unborn, who supply an equivalent sum, to take up certificates of the expenses paid by the living.[168]

Indeed, Taylor adds:

> Nothing exposed the American and French Revo-
> lutions to greater danger, than the attempts to use

---

168   Taylor, *Inquiry*, 234.

this delusion. Anticipation was tried, it taxed the existing generations by depreciation, it superseded the cultivation of other modes of putting energies in motion, it failed, the failure almost obliterated the memory and suspended the use, of the real means of war, and a dangerous crisis in both cases was produced... Political and religious opinion, and a love of country, are stronger excitements of existing warlike energies, than anticipation. They cannot be stolen or hoarded; but war carried on by paper, is starved by peculation, and produces the utmost degree of publick expense, with the least degree of publick spirit.[169]

In taking this view of debt-financed warfare, Taylor nicely anticipated the views of the American economist H. J. Davenport, writing just after World War I.[170] As for Taylor's antimilitarism, it was not the same thing as being unwilling or afraid to fight. The point was to fight only when absolutely essential. Otherwise, we courted the fate of the "European nations" which "exist for the benefit of armies and navies" and where "armies and navies do not exist for their benefit."[171]

Britain: The Negative Role Model

For Taylor the moral was clear: Americans must take action to uproot the new class of subsidized capitalists or suffer the fate of England. Britain served as Taylor's negative role model, whose evils — empire and domestic oppression — were intimately related. Taylor paints this rather unflattering picture:

In contemplating the example of England, we must discern compulsion at the beginning, as well as at

---

169 *Ibid.*, 236

170 H. J. Davenport, "The War-Tax Paradox," *American Economic Review*, 9 (March 1919), 34-46.

171 Taylor, *Construction Construed*, 334.

WAR, PEACE, AND EMPIRE

the end of her commerce. Her labour is compelled
to sell low to her mercantile interest, and foreign
nations or her colonies are compelled to purchase
high of the same interest. Her maritime power is
the instrument of the latter compulsion, and her
bank currency of the former. This bank currency
cannot force up the prices in foreign nations, as her
fleet does by vexing and crippling competition; but
it can force down the prices of labour at home. By
taxing labour to maintain this fleet, that commerce
is enabled to sell high abroad; and by a monopolized
currency, regulating the prices of domestick labour,
she buys low at home. She draws wealth and opu-
lence from two sources, knavery and violence. To
maintain the oppression over foreign nations and
colonies, she frequently involves herself in war; to
maintain the oppression over home labour, she is
forced to use the penalties, corruptions, and merce-
nary armies, forming the code of all despotisms. But
she is enriched, because labour is her slave; goad-
ed by a paper system, and she makes competition
shrink by a fleet.[172]

The relative internal freedom of Britain was little comfort to its
dependencies:

> Mr. Hume has said that free governments are most
> happy for those who partake of their freedom, but
> most ruinous and oppressive to their provinces.
> They dispense ruin and oppression to provinces,
> as the inevitable effect of a separate interest. The

---

172   Taylor, *Inquiry*, 311-312.

certainty of this moral law, is nearly demonstrated in the relations between England and Ireland, and quite so in India.[173]

In the United States, the "vicious principle of creating wealth by law" and a knavish submission "to party despotism" had between them made elections "more contemptible than in England" and a "cross patronage between the president and congress" had made other evils worse.[174] On the other hand, "Our [ideal republican] policy has attempted to wrest war from the hands of executive power, lest it should be used as a means of making legislation an instrument for advancing its projects, and representation a mask to conceal them. War is the keenest carving knife for cutting up nations into delicious morsels for parties and their leaders." Further, war "swells a few people to enormous size," "puts arms into the hands of ambition, avarice, pride, and self-love," and "breeds a race of men, nominally heroes, mistaken for patriots, and really tyrants." Finally, under the superstitions and corruptions of the party system, a mere 26% of the legislature, by controlling a 51% majority, "holds in fact the power of declaring war," while acting the part of "a genuine republican majority."[175]

Under this mistaken and centralizing version of republicanism, patronage becomes a mode "of destroying forms of government, by civil law" and "corrupts by hope, by fruition, and by disappointment." A point is reached, not far off, where, "Accumulated, patronage becomes the real legislator of a nation"; under a cloud of "secrecy, both legislative and executive" for which pretenses "can never be wanting..." Alluding to what we would now call "national security," Taylor writes:

> Secrecy is good for conquest, say its advocates. Let nations who wish to be free, remember that freedom cannot exist, except by controlling *the conquests*

---

173 *Ibid.*, 491. I hardly need to hammer away at contemporary parallels.

174 *Ibid.*, 505-507.

175 *Ibid.*, 508-510 (inset quotation at 508).

of their own governments at home. Patronage
and secrecy united, are daily carrying some of
their defences. Conquests abroad are rare, and no
compensation for conquest at home.[176]

Empire and Oligarchy

Now Taylor turns to the *structural logic* of empire. In his
view, the English state amounted to "a confederation of parties
of interest," excluding the people and consisting of "the church
of England, the paper stock party, the East India company, the
military party, the pensioned and sinecure party, and the ins
and outs, once called whigs and tories" — all under the umbrella
of the legal monarchy. Since this coalition constituted the state,
the English nation as such had "no government" and "no British
nation" existed but for these interest groups.[177]

Taylor notes the advocacy of "a brisk circulation of money" by
Dr. Samuel Johnson, "the best informed tory," adding his usual
remarks on the ills of paper inflation. Analogously, Taylor writes,
"a brisk circulation of power is also produced. Accumulated in a few
hands, like money, it breaks down confinement, spreads itself far
and wide," repaying the general public much as paper does, that is,
badly. Dr. Johnson has "neglected to tell us... that money attracts
power, and power, money; and that by accumulating either for the
sake of a brisk circulation, you accumulate and circulate both."[178]

This seems a good example of Taylor's sociopolitical acumen
and his ability to spell out interrelations among various social phe-
nomena. But there is more, as Taylor undermines two arguments

---

176   *Ibid.*, 539 – 540.

177   *Ibid.*, 547-549. Cf. E. P. Thompson on 18th-century Britain: "This was a predatory phase of
agrarian and commercial capitalism, and the State was itself among the prime objects of prey..."
With the Hanoverian monarchs came "a new set of courtier-brigands.... and the real killings were
to be made in the distribution, cornering and sale of goods or raw materials... in the manipulation
of credit, and in the seizure of the offices of State." "Eighteenth-century English society: class struggle
without class?" *Social History*, 3 (May 1978), 139.

178   Taylor, *Inquiry*, 550-551. On the brisk circulation of power, see Tom Burns,
"Sovereignty, Interests and Bureaucracy in the Modern State," *British Journal of Sociology*, 31
(December 1980), 494-495.

advanced in favor of large accumulations of power: "uniformity of religion" and "the difficulty of governing an extensive territory." Europe had given up the first, and America the second as far as outright monarchy was concerned. But practical knowledge is widely dispersed over a large territory and this "moral geometry" limits the "knowledge and will" of a king. Hence,

> When the territory bursts beyond his orbit, monarchy ceases and some anomalous government ensues; oligarchical, military, deputy-royal, tumultuous, or infinitely variegated by circumstances. Hence neither the virtues nor vices of a monarch are felt at a distance from his person.... monarchy ends at the end of the monarch's sphere.

"Monarchy only succeeds," Taylor says, in cases of appropriate scale, as in "armies, garrisons, savage tribes and private families"; in a wider sphere, the monarch has in fact a mere "power of changing oligarchs." This brings the analysis back to presidential patronage, "which must depend upon the knowledge and will of the very worst kind of oligarchs; such as are irresponsible and unknown." This may indeed be a form of government, but it is neither a republic nor a proper monarchy. Hence, where a republic and a monarchy "both exercise the tyrannical power of distributing wealth, the latter must be least oppressive, because it is less expensive to gratify the rapaciousness of one, than of many," for "spurious republicks... universally afflict the people with the heaviest taxes."[179]

America's federal distribution of power had provided the means of warding off such dangers. But the party system and available executive patronage favored oligarchic practice, while vaguely drawn presidential power and ongoing usurpation fostered wars, which extended the reach of patronage and power both economically and geographically. Here, Taylor's domestic and foreign policy concerns are joined.

---

179   Taylor, *Inquiry*, 551-553.

Where foreign relations and security are concerned, Taylor will not yield to claims of ironclad "realist" necessity. *We Americans* do not have to do these things, he says. We were able to resist the European system "more successfully than any other nation":

> Extent keeps at a distance from the bulk of the nation the calamities of war, and enables it to reflect. Cut up into sections, not a single individual might escape them. Small nations are continually exposed to the artifice of legal wars... But a nation possessed of extensive territory, happily removed from real causes of collision with other nations, like the United States, is peculiarly favoured by providence for the detection of this artifice...[180]

America, governed as a monarchy, in fact if not in name, would "only retain the advantage of extensive territory, by an oligarchy composed of deputy-kings, bashaws, satraps or mandarins." As a decentralized republican confederation, with genuine self-government in its members, the United States might expand indefinitely and "unite the most extensive territories by justice..." Taylor envisioned "forming a great nation, by a chain of republicks...."[181]

This is certainly a straightforward statement of an "isolationism" or non-interventionism grounded on strict republicanism.[182] On Taylor's view, then, we were not "free-riding" on the British navy, which — according to many 20th-century scholars — was benevolently shielding us from foreign danger. Only Americans themselves could undermine their fortunate geographical and political circumstances.

---

180   *Ibid.*, 554.

181   *Ibid.*, 554-555.

182   See also Taylor, *Tyranny Unmasked*, 125-125, 266 (esp. 125). Taylor shared this unconcern about foreign danger with the ill-starred Antifederalists; see Jonathan Marshall, "Empire or Liberty: The Antifederalists and Foreign Policy, 1787-1788," *Journal of Libertarian Studies*, 4 (Summer 1980), 233-254.

The Balance of Power

It is no surprise that John Taylor, who denied that the laws of nations could of themselves confer sovereignty on any American government, was also skeptical about the doctrine of the balance of power. In this, he agreed with a good many liberals from Kant to Cobden and Bright. As he put it:

> What is the political attitude of nations toward each other, supposed by a balance of power? Hostility. What is the effect of hostility? War. A balance of power is therefore the most complete invention imaginable for involving one combination of states, in a war with another.[183]

Nor was Taylor much taken with a parallel idea: the "balance of trade."[184] Not surprisingly, Taylor's main interest in balance of power doctrines pertained to the American union of states. Because of the Missouri Compromise, he had begun to worry that geographical blocs within the union would summon up a balancing doctrine as fraught with evils as the European theory. Here the balance would obtain between "slave" and "free" states. But balance-of-power politics would lead to political tinkering and brokering outside the scope of the constitution, and a sustained campaign by antislavery philanthropists against the South as a bloc "would certainly destroy the union."[185]

Taylor foresees "civil" war, with massive death and destruction. He makes an ironic aside about how the reformers might crusade in another venue: "if our consciences tell us that we ought to enslave freemen,[186] to make slaves free, and to cause the destruction of a million or two of people, white and black, in the good work, nature

---

183   Taylor, *Construction Construed*, 291. Cf. A. F. Pollard, "The Balance of Power," *Journal of the British Institute of International Affairs*, 2 (March 1923), 51-64.

184   Taylor, *Tyranny Unmasked*, 18 and ff.

185   Taylor, *Construction Construed*, 293.

186   Compare the title of Jeffrey Rogers Hummel's book: *Emancipating Slaves, Enslaving Free Men* (Chicago: Open Court, 1996).

tells us to give the preference in such favours, to those who need them most" — perhaps in Brazil, Cuba, or Africa. Nevertheless, Taylor was so far from being a "disunionist" in any positive sense that, in describing the geographical immunities of the United States, he attributed Americans' safety to maintaining a union of some kind. But he was not an unconditional unionist. Instead, he cited "the natural right of self-defence" as the South's guide, should those states be pressed too hard on the subject of slavery.[187]

The Treaty-Making Power

The treaty power has long been prized and feared as a source of new and unknowable federal powers. As late as the mid-1950s, a popular movement sought to define and curtail that power by means of the Bricker Amendment. It took all the leverage of the Eisenhower administration to defeat the proposal in the Senate by one vote. Taylor addresses the matter as follows:

> .... [N]o additional personal or spherical power was conferred by declaring the laws and treaties to be also the supreme law of the land.... The declaration, that the constitution was the supreme law of the land, confirmed all its limitations, divisions, restrictions and limitations of power, and it never was intended that either should be altered in the least degree by laws or treaties, or be placed under the power of those who should make laws or treaties. On the contrary, the laws were to be made in pursuance of the constitution, and the treaties, under the authority of the United States. The United States have no authority, except that which is given by the constitution. Both the laws and treaties to be supreme must, therefore, be made in conformity

---

187   Taylor, *Construction Construed*, 293, 314. The noted American student of international law John Bassett Moore saw the war of 1861-1865 as "the result of a contest over the balance of power..." Quoted in Ernst B. Haas, "The Balance of Power: Prescription, Concept, or Propaganda," *World Politics*, 5 (July 1953), 452.

with the powers bestowed, limited and reserved by the constitution, and by these we must determine whether a law or a treaty has been constitutionally made, before the question of its supremacy can occur.[188]

Further:

The first instance of a spherical supremacy which I recollect, was the claim of the treaty-making power, to bind the taxing or legislative power, by stipulating in a treaty for the payment of money. This was a dispute between two federal political spheres; but the principles, upon which it has been or must be settled, are those by which the rights of the federal and state political spheres can alone be ascertained.... As the federal legislative sphere may justly deny to the treaty-making power, a right to abridge the powers delegated to itself by the constitution, under a claim of supremacy, or by any species of construction; so, the state spheres may justly deny to the federal legislative or judicial spheres, a right to abridge by similar modes the powers reserved to them. Suppose the treaty-making power should stipulate with England to declare war against France; would that deprive congress of the right of preserving peace, with which it is invested by the constitution?[189]

---

188 Taylor, *Construction Construed*, 124.

189 *Ibid.*, 137.

Taylor's observations on foreign affairs comport well with these comments by Andrew Lytle on the period of Jefferson's and Madison's rule:

> The rub lay in the nature of foreign affairs which, by the crises arising out of world conditions, are able to subvert the best constitutions and reduce the ordering of the internal affairs of a union to the support of a foreign policy which may bring distress, suffering, and revolution. It was not long before New England was asked, on account of foreign policy, to acquiesce patriotically to laws dealing injuries and ruin.[190]

---

190   Lytle, "John Taylor," 60-61.

Part V.

JOHN TAYLOR OF CAROLINE,
LIBERAL, RADICAL, REACTIONARY

Taylor as a Liberal "Individualist"

TAYLOR WRITES that society not made up of individuals is a pointless abstraction:

> Society exclusively of individuals, is an ideal being, as metaphysical as the idea of a triangle. If a number of people should inclose themselves within a triangle, they would hear with great astonishment, that they had lost the power of changing the form of the inclosure; and that the dead form of the triangle governed living beings, instead of living beings who created that figure, governing it.[191]

Taylor is not trying to do without law, social order, intermediate institutions, or even virtue in the ordinary sense of the term, but he is trying to prevent our being locked beforehand into *political* institutions beyond the reach of alteration, starting with the federal union. Taylor was also at pains to discredit those *artificial*

---

191 Taylor, *Inquiry*, 148.

intermediate orders or legally supported castes championed by Adams, which we may easily distinguish from the sociological notion of naturally occurring intermediate institutions.[192]

Taylor certainly expounded a kind of methodological individualism characteristic of the liberal thought of his time. As Michael O'Brien puts it: "Perhaps no Southern thinker was more radically invested in the idea of individualism...." Thus, Taylor considered "society a reification." This leads, it would seem, to a certain contradiction: if states, federations, and so on, were entirely artificial constructions, then "society" in Taylor's usage might itself seem equally artificial.[193] At bottom, however, Taylor does not appear to believe this. Even so, the critique Taylor makes of systems he opposes seems more solid than the grounding he chooses for his own positive conception of social order.

In any case, writers who wish to deny Taylor's standing as a liberal, individualist, or democrat because his "social background 'determined' his political theory" are denying that he could write what he wrote.[194] But he did write it. Perhaps someone in Taylor's position *should* have held different views for various reasons, but that is another matter.

Even so, it hardly seems satisfactory to leave Taylor as the Thomas Paine or Henry David Thoreau of Hazelwood. First, it may be that political analysis grounded on individuals — as a matter of method — does not automatically entail antisocial conclusions. Next, Taylor could (and did) simply take society as he knew it as largely given. In practice, then, Taylor's vision of society would resemble what Richard M. Weaver called "social-bond individualism," which "battles unremittingly for individual rights, while recognizing that these have to be secured within the social context," and knows that "the battle must be fought within the

---

192   Taylor, *Construction Construed*, 19.

193   O'Brien, *Conjectures of Order*, II, 791; and see Yehoshua Arieli, *Individualism and Nationalism in American Ideology* (Baltimore: Penguin Books, 1964), 166-178, for a convincing account of Taylor's individualist premises.

194   Gillis J. Harp, "Taylor, Calhoun, and the Decline of Theory of Political Disharmony," *Journal of the History of Ideas*, 46 (January 1985), 111 note.

community, not outside the community and not through means that would in effect deny all political organization."[195]

Third, there was religion, which Taylor could leave in the background since there was in his kind of political liberalism no conflict with Protestantism. Indeed, in his day, American liberalism and Protestantism shared the same historical narrative. Taylor frequently and violently criticized "hierarchy" — identified with the medieval Catholic order — and equated it rhetorically with the Federalists' paper-feudalism. But if Protestantism reinforced a certain kind of individualism in Taylor and others, it was not individualism without any community at all. Overall, then, Taylor's applied views call to mind the Protestant conservatism of Wilhelm Röpke, a free-market economist with considerable interest in intermediate and local institutions.[196] Unlike Röpke, Taylor did not spend much time on intermediate institutions (other than the states), since in his time and place, those still seemed sufficiently intact to be assumed into the background.

Taylor as an Agrarian

Historians have called John Taylor an agrarian liberal or democrat and a prophet of secession. As noted, Williams saw him as a "physiocrat" who sought to realize a Southern feudal utopia by way of *laissez faire* economics.[197] None of these labels adequately describes him. Taylor loved the land, but cannot be confined to the historians' conventionally narrow agrarian box.

---

195   Richard M. Weaver, "Two Types of American Individualism," in George M. Curtis III and James J. Thompson, Jr., eds., *The Southern Essays of Richard M. Weaver* (Indianapolis, IN: Liberty Press, 1987), 82. For the ways that slavery might have reinforced the personal libertarianism of Southern whites, see Edmund S. Morgan, *American Slavery, American Freedom: The Ordeal of Colonial Virginia* (New York: W. W. Norton & Co., 1975).

196   See John Zmirak, *Wilhelm Röpke: Swiss Localist, Global Economist* (Wilmington, DE: ISI Books, 2001).

197   Williams' use of "feudal" in this context (*Contours of American History*, 151-153) makes it rather equivalent to "Country" in Pocock's terms. The Marxist legal historian Mitchell Franklin, with much verbal abuse, equated federal and feudal in "Concerning the Influence of Roman Law on the Formation of the Constitution of the United States," *Nature, Society, and Thought*, 16 (2003), 405-438 (first published in 1964), while Marxist historians Eugene D. Genovese and Elisabeth Fox-Genovese have observed that physiocratic ideas "cannot usefully be read as medieval or reactionary..." *Fruits of Merchant Capital* (New York: Oxford, 1983), 280.

In his introduction to *Arator* (1977), M. E. Bradford calls Taylor "a Virginia Cato," and sees him as revealing "the 'patriarchal' side of his mind" in that book. He writes, "Reasoning after the fact, from history, Taylor denies that government and society are necessarily one." In all this, says Bradford, Taylor reasoned from historical materials and not *a priori*, whatever his occasional remarks on natural rights might mean.[198] Indeed, Bradford believes that underneath his 18th-century liberal language, Taylor — influenced, like his contemporaries, by classical Roman models — was in the last instance a defender of those republics that are "closed, rural, religious, and corporate societies."

Such a republic need not be *anti*-commercial, but it did not define its purpose as primarily commercial, nor did it see the state's role as that of broker, promoter, and subsidizer of business enterprise. The state's role was to provide justice and security in a society already formed, not to make the economy go or to reform society according to blueprint. The achievements of the American Revolution, embodied in local self-government under the Articles of Confederation, "forestalled the instability inherent in the 'balance-of-power' regimes praised in commercial republican theory: in regimes where the guarantees of order are converted by natural declension into the engines of exploitation."[199] Bradford's insight cuts through some of the debris left behind by republican-school historians and suggests that many figures classified as modernizing liberals were deeply indebted to a "Venetian" model of commercial republicanism requiring an imperial and mercantilist state — the "republic for increase" of Machiavelli and Harrington.[200]

In Taylor's writings, agrarian themes appear frequently, but unlike Jefferson he never asked to be "on the footing of China,"[201] that is, to live in a literally "isolated" agrarian state. For Taylor's society was *already* agrarian and this fact goes far

---

198   Bradford, "A Virginia Cato," 39, 33.

199   Bradford, 18-21.

200   Pocock, *Machiavellian Moment*, 391-393, 510-511 ("commonwealth for expansion").

201   For Jefferson's comment about China, see William Grampp, "A Re-examination of Jeffersonian Economics," *Southern Economic Journal*, 12 (January 1946), 269.

toward explaining why he felt no need to speak as a conservative or communitarian. He wrote that American landowners — "as a majority, and incapable of subsisting upon any other interest" — could not be an aristocratic order.[202]

Taylor believed that his "policy" of political liberalism ("republicanism") would allow agrarian communities to flourish, if carried out within a decentralized political order. And now we seem to find ourselves in the 1920s and 1930s, with Vernon Louis Parrington, J. Allen Smith, and (to a lesser extent) Charles A. Beard, and see that agrarians were perhaps liberals of a kind. But how do we (or Taylor) get anyone to go along with *this* liberalism instead of five or six other programs also called "liberalism"? Here the Hartz problem returns. The modern liberal Hartz read American history through left-of-center glasses. He concluded that given the absence of real feudalism in America, Americans had always tended to be Lockean liberals. Hartz was not entirely happy about this "fact." He took it to mean that thinkers like Taylor were either defending a nonexistent feudalism or foolishly trying to establish it under impossible social conditions. Naturally, such fellows ended up as fringe agitators ancestral to the John Birchers.

Hartz's reading ignored the many substantive issues Taylor addressed and was entirely too convenient for modernizing liberals. Yet owing to inherited categories, we are still overcoming false alternatives put forward in the mid-20th century. Even the "republican paradigm" of recent memory (ca. 1955-1990) was superimposed on existing false alternatives, thereby robbing it of what real merit it had.[203] (There is a price for insisting that decentralization is feudal — and *only* feudal.[204])

---

202   Taylor, *Inquiry*, 478.

203   Cf. Colin Gordon, "Crafting a Usable Past: Consensus, Ideology, and Historians of the American Revolution," *William & Mary Quarterly*, 46 (October 1989), 671-695.

204   Here Wilhelm Röpke's sharp distinction between seigneurial (lordly) and communal decentralization under "feudalism" becomes extremely important. See *Civitas Humana: A Humane Order of Society* (London: William Hodge & Co., 1948), 106-112.

Even if we choose to remain with Hartz *inside* a vaguely defined American liberalism, that outlook was broad enough in itself to provide us with many serious internal struggles, mistaken analyses, and competing strategies. Lytle faults Taylor and his allies for "believing and acting upon the belief that the Constitution, a political contract, could take the place of all those traditional institutions which make for an abundant and complete life..." He chalks this failing up to "the contradictions which Republican liberalism subjected him...." Indeed, "Taylor's predicament was common to most of the early Republicans: conservative instincts and desires coupled with liberal intellectual principles."[205]

Referring to *Tyranny Unmasked*, Lytle noted that Taylor "makes the philosophical defense of agrarianism; but it is because it is a philosophical defense that it fails." Taylor's argument against centralization was sound, "but like Jefferson, he fails to offer a medium by which the bad may be destroyed and the good set up and maintained." He adds:

> [Taylor] can only appeal to the intelligence of the voter for the remedy. Liberalism inevitably used the terms good and bad. It needed, as a fighting cry, virtue triumphing over evil. Cromwell's leadership was shrewder. He did not concentrate on discussions of the morality of the Stuarts. He threw his Ironsides against the devil's agents.[206]

Lytle, speaking from an organic sense of Southern society across time, more than implies that Southern statesmen, including Taylor, might have better served their society by calculating the *value of the union* much sooner than they did. Lytle, who was trying to write from outside liberalism, had little sympathy for Taylor's liberal moments. Lytle's point dovetails somewhat with Gordon Wood's complaint that despite Taylor's rhetorical victory over John Adams in the *Inquiry*, Adams did have something to say after all. Taylor

---

205   Lytle, "John Taylor of Caroline," 75, 63, 58.

206   Lytle, "Backwoods Progression," 86.

urged that good institutions would overcome "avariciousness," but he does not seem to explain why the avaricious would permit those institutional structures to survive. His lifelong project was, after all, one of showing how much they were threatened.[207] As a result, his laborious works served to demonstrate *precisely how* his opponents had overthrown his hope that unalloyed "interest" might "secure the fidelity of nations to themselves."[208] Taylor's easy dismissal of virtue had a place, no doubt, in his polemic against John Adams. But virtue, repressed in theory, will come back, perhaps in distorted form.[209] Taylor was relying, in fact, on inherited virtues — Christian, societal, even political — while attempting to do without them at a foundational level.

A Note on Economic Development under Agrarian Republicanism

Taking John Taylor as a key critic of America's main political-economic drift, we must briefly address the question of economic development under Taylor's program. In a country that believes in unceasing material progress, the charge that Taylor's ideas would have slowed growth and mechanization seems damning. The noted historian Henry Bamford Parkes writes: "In a country governed in accordance with agrarian ideals, manufacturing could have developed only very slowly, since there would have been no large accumulations of capital and no supplies of cheap labor."[210] Many, perhaps most, Americans had another vision — one of rapid growth and universal prosperity — and took national banking, "internal improvements," and other such measures as the best route to the general welfare so defined.

---

207   Wood, *Creation of the American Republic*, 591-592. Giving Adams's "realism" about human its due, it does not follow that his specific recommendations were superior to Taylor's.

208   Taylor, *Inquiry*, 161.

209   Harvey C. Mansfield, *Machiavelli's Virtue* (Chicago: University of Chicago Press, 1998 [1966]) comes to mind.

210   Henry Bamford Parkes, *The American Experience* (New York: Vintage Books, 1959 [1947]), 119.

French economic historian Paul Mantoux wrote (1947) of the English enclosure movement, that if "the bulk of the rural population [had] remained on the land the triumph of the factory system might have come later, but it could not have been indefinitely postponed, as is shown conclusively by what took place in France."[211] Now the alleged impossibility of "modernization" under republican *laissez faire* recedes to manageable proportions. We could add (as Taylor would have) that this other path to modernization might have been more natural, organic, and less chaotic than the actual route followed. To be told endlessly, after the fact, that the 19th-century American "road to capitalism" was inevitable in all its details, is to add insult to injury. It was only as inevitable as the victory of Northern armies serving as the vanguard of Lincoln's developmental coalition of northeastern industrialists and western farmers.[212]

Noting the similar views on economic concentration held by both "conservatives" like Theodore Roosevelt and sundry Marxists, the neo-republican critic Walter Karp observes:

> The political distortions engendered by class analysis [are] well illustrated in a common ideological treatment of America's small farmers. Since they, like small businessmen, were antimonopoly, they have often been categorized as "capitalists." One result of this is that the great Populist revolt against the party machines is often described as "essentially conservative." This is because "small capitalists," by ideological definition, are in the backwash of

---

211   Paul Mantoux, *The Industrial Revolution in the Eighteenth Century* (New York: Harper & Row, 1961 [1928]), 184.

212   With the federal government overseeing the "primitive accumulation" of land through Indian wars, a bad example already existed, which made it unlikely that a non-mercantilist policy could ever be politically popular. See Ronald Takaki, *Iron Cages: Race and Culture in 19th Century America* (New York: Oxford University Press, 1990 [1979]), "Primitive Accumulation," 69-79. Cf. Richard Franklin Bensel, *Yankee Leviathan: The Origins of Central State Authority in America, 1859-1877* (New York: Cambridge University Press, 1990), Ch. 7, "Southern Separatism and the Class Basis of American Politics."

history trying to "hold back social change," a mealy-mouthed way of saying that the oligarchs were trying to get rid of them.

Karp adds: "Ideological categories always describe as natural, inevitable or inherent what the wielders of corrupt power are actively trying to accomplish."[213] Taylor knew this and never shied away from stating just *who it was* that was bringing about so much "inevitable social change." All this might be taken a step farther. Recent discussions of small-scale production as an alternative to modernization from above suggest it was possible not merely *to delay* industrialization, as Mantoux wrote, but to confine it within a quite different social framework.[214]

The Continuing Relevance of John Taylor of Caroline

We have seen that for John Taylor, men were a blend of good and evil, guided by self-interest, whose political relations worked best in the right institutional framework. Rejecting archaic republicanism and transcending the old "checks and balances" and simple "separation of powers," Taylor aimed at *breaking power up* geographically and functionally, thereby preventing the establishment of effective tyranny. He believed in an individually held "right of self government," which made possible the cooperative creation of governments as responsible agents. In practice, he located self-government ("sovereignty") in the peoples of the states ("state-nations") and not in a fancied, aggregated people of the

---

213   Walter Karp, *Indispensable Enemies: The Politics of Misrule in America* (Baltimore: Penguin Books, 1974), 179 note.

214   See Robert Brenner, "The Origins of Capitalist Development: A Critique of Neo-Smithian Marxism," *New Left Review*, 104 (July-August 1977), 25-92, esp. 88-90; Arthur Di Quattro, "The Labor Theory of Value and Simple Commodity Production," *Science & Society*, 71 (October 2007), 455-483; Harriet Friedmann, "World Market, State, and Family Farm: Social Bases of Household Production in the Era of Wage Labor," *Comparative Studies in History and Society*, 20 (October 1978), 545-586; R. Cole Harris, "The Simplification of Europe Overseas," *Annals of the Association of American Geographers*, 67 (December 1977), 469-483; Claudio Katz, "Karl Marx on the transition from feudalism to capitalism," *Theory and Society*, 22 (June 1993), 363-389, and "Thomas Jefferson's Liberal Anticapitalism," *American Journal of Political Science,* 47 (January 2003), 1-17; and William Lazonick, "Karl Marx and Enclosures in England," *Review of Radical Political Economics*, 6 (1974), 1-59. And see the massive treatise by Kevin Carson, *Organization Theory: A Libertarian Perspective* (Booksurge, 2009).

United States. Summarizing his views, Taylor wrote: "Our policy divides power, and unites the nation in one interest; Mr. Adams's divides a nation into several interests and unites power."[215]

Taylor denied that virtuous or vicious popular character as such produced "factions" aiming at overthrowing the public good. As Grant McConnell notes, rather than arrange a constitution (like Madison) to mitigate "the *effects* of factionalism," Taylor sought "to remove [its] *causes*." Class struggle resulted from unjust legislation and especially from arbitrary transfers of property. Taylor's remedy, as summarized by McConnell, was:

> Remove the legal base from under the stock jobbers, the banks, the paper money party, the tariff-supported manufacturers, and so on; destroy the system of patronage by which the executive has corrupted the legislature; bring down the usurped authority of the Supreme Court.[216]

This analysis greatly resembled that of English and French radical liberals and English Ricardian socialists. In their view, governments were unproductive and must be kept to a minimum; minimally regulated markets could better provide for society's economic needs. Taylor's program of divided power, substantive limits, and constitutional strict construction by the concerned parties (and not just one federal court) would stifle faction from the outset. With faction already denied any property-transferring powers, the republic need not expand geographically — certainly not just to "dilute" factions. And a non-expansionist policy was good on other grounds, since expansion could undermine free institutions through aggressive wars, standing armies, debt, and taxes — an array of Court policies amounting to mercantilism and empire.[217] Because Taylor wanted to sustain and perfect American

---

215 Taylor, *Inquiry*, 378.

216   McConnell, "John Taylor and the Democratic Tradition," 27.

217   Cf. Bradford, "A Virginia Cato," 26-27.

republicanism, he had no room for Jefferson's compromises and firmly opposed the mercantilism of Madison and other latter-day Republicans.

Taylor's ideas enjoyed renewed attention when the Jacksonian movement rose up against the all-Federalist-all-Republican synthesis of the Era of Good Feeling. He was a prophet for hard-money and free-trade advocates like the Benton brothers and William Leggett — a Northern Jacksonian and "an unconditional, almost obsessive advocate of laissez faire." Leggett, indeed, thought that hard money, free trade, and *laissez faire* positively promoted an agrarian society.[218]

In Taylor's political economy, artificial aristocracies (paper or otherwise) can only sustain their projects in the long run through some form of despotism.[219] Late 18th-century critics often characterized what they opposed as consolidation, empire, or monarchy. As Thomas Paine put it, "monarchy is the knot that ties the robber's bundle." The monarchy feared by Taylor, Antifederalists, and republicans, is indeed upon us — a plebiscitary and illegitimate thing, which entrusts the temporary occupant of the mighty presidential office with powers beyond the ken of any great historical despot. As J.G.A. Pocock has written:

> Democratic federalism grew into the greatest empire
> of patronage and influence the world has ever known,
> and remains to this day dedicated to the principle
> that politics cannot work unless politicians do things
> for their friends and their friends know where to
> find them. New democrat is but old Whig writ large;
> and the Federal Constitution, that great triumph
> of the eighteenth-century political art, seems to
> have perpetuated the eighteenth-century world

---

218   Leggett, as characterized by Marvin Meyers, *The Jacksonian Persuasion: Politics and Belief* (New York: Vintage Books, 1960), 185-205, quotation at 186.

219   Cf. John Law's "System" as described in Kaiser, "Money, Despotism, and Public Opinion," in aid of which the French state tried to control prices, opinion, and all of commerce merely to sustain a doomed inflationary enterprise (see Note 65).

it was designed to deal with.... America may have guaranteed the survival of the forms of corruption it was created to resist.[220]

This suggests that we have a problem on our hands. Do we have the materials, somewhere in American traditions, with which to meet it — "Country-party ideas" perhaps? Some might say, no. Historian Roland Berthoff, for example, sees the "prolonged domination of the American mind by an outmoded theory of politics as a great tragedy."[221] But if we are *dominated* by these outmoded ideas — whether "republican," "liberal," or both — why do we never get corresponding *policies*? Why do we get instead the tragedy of American diplomacy as narrated by Williams and the corruption described by Pocock? In quest of answers, Taylor's critique of actually existing American capitalism could prove very useful.

It might be added that the new social history of American economic life, which emerged in the late 1980s, is quite consistent with Taylor's understanding of his time. The historians in question (see note 222) agree that between 1790 and 1830 America underwent a transition from self-contained, largely local economies and markets to a new "national" and increasingly unified market economy under rules favorable to capitalist development.[222] Further, recent writing (chiefly Marxist) on "small commodity production" as a mode of production separate from capitalism is very much to the point. And where was this mode found? Precisely in North America (and similar colonial environments) in the period specified by the new social historians and precisely the period of Taylor's work. Finally, the work of certain Marxist

---

220   J.G.A. Pocock, "1776: The Revolution against Parliament," in Pocock, ed., *Three British Revolutions: 1641, 1688, 1776* (Princeton, NJ: Princeton University Press, 1980), 286.

221   Berthoff, as characterized by Daniel Walker Howe, "European Sources of Political Ideas in Jeffersonian America," *Reviews in American History*, 10 (December 1982), 35.

222   See Edward Countryman, "Of Republicanism, Capitalism, and the 'American Mind,'" *William & Mary Quarterly*, 44 (July 1987), 556-562; Paul A. Gilje, "The Rise of Capitalism in the Early Republic," *Journal of the Early Republic*, 16 (September 1996), 159-181; Colin Gordon, "Crafting a Usable Past," *WMQ*, 46 (October 1989), 671-695; Allan Kulikoff, "The Transition to Capitalism in Rural America," *WMQ*, 46 (January 1989), 120-144, and "Households and Markets: Toward a New Synthesis of American Agrarian History," *WMQ*, 50 (April 1993), 342-355; [and] Michael Merrill, "Putting 'Capitalism' in Its Place: A Review of Recent Literature," *WMQ*, 52 (April 1995), 317-326.

legal historians[223] reinforces an obvious interpretive convergence: what drove the "transition" from a modest scale of economic life to the economics of continental enormity was the new political and legal order instituted by the Federalist movement; the resulting economy was largely what the Federalist vanguard consciously intended. The constitution, under their constructive reading, was the anvil of this "social change." Charles Beard told us as much.[224] It is too soon to say whether an historiographical coalition of small-commodity theorists, pro-peasant Marxists, the heirs of Beard, agrarians, and others is on the horizon, but if so, it would have its uses.

I would only add that we could have avoided many vexed questions and false alternatives, had even a few American historians made Taylor's definitions of parties and fundamental issues (especially in *New Views*) into organizing principles of their work. It is true that judged as a way of reading the constitution or as a model of politics, Taylor's thought "failed." But it has its value as a critical benchmark, a standard by which to measure what has happened to us since. Despite the many epithets — "nostalgia," "reaction," "agrarianism," "provincialism" — there remains in Taylor a hard core of intelligent and rigorous analysis of economic and political institutions and the follies of mankind.

---

223   E.g., Morton J. Horwitz, "The Rise of Legal Formalism," *American Journal of Legal History*, 19 (October 1975), 251-264. Wythe Holt, "'To Establish Justice': Politics and the Judiciary Act of 1789, and the Invention of the Federal Courts," *Duke Law Journal*, 1989 (December 1989), 1421-1531. (In some of Holt's work, he is a virtual states-rights Marxist.) For Small Commodity Production see the sources in note 214.

224   Charles A. Beard, *An Economic Interpretation of the Constitution of the United States* (New York: Free Press, 1965 [1913]), Chapter 6, "The Constitution as an Economic Document." Cf. Albert Jay Nock, *Jefferson* (Washington, DC: National Home Library Foundation, 1926) and *Our Enemy the State* (New York: Free Life Editions, 1973 [1935]).

ABOUT THE AUTHOR

JOSEPH R. STROMBERG is an independent historian born in southwest Florida and currently living in northeastern Georgia. He holds a B.A. and M.A. in History (Florida Atlantic University 1970, 1971) and did further graduate work at the University of Florida (1973-75). He was a Richard M. Weaver Fellow (1970-1971) and has taught college courses in World Civilizations and American History as an adjunct instructor. His writing has appeared in the *Journal of Libertarian Studies, Telos, Chronicles, The Freeman, Future of Freedom, Independent Review,* and *The American Conservative.* He has contributed essays to various collections including *Secession, State, and Liberty (1998)* and *Opposing the Crusader State* (2007) and has written for Antiwar.com (1999-2003), the Abbeville Institute, Reckonin', and other websites.

Alongside those activities, he worked 35 years or so in carpentry. He has family in Georgia, North Carolina, Colorado, Utah, Arizona, and Nevada, including five grandchildren.

BEST SELLERS AND NEW RELEASES

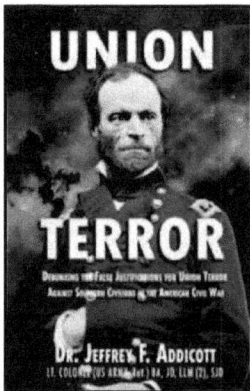

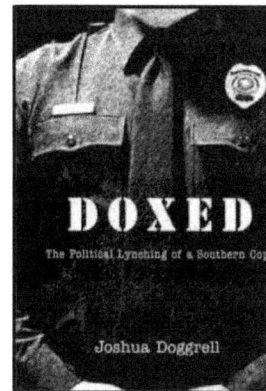

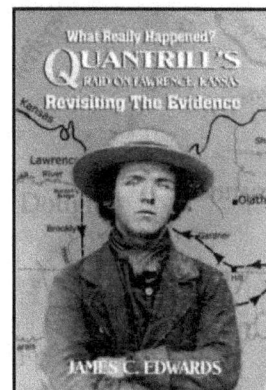

OVER 90 TITLES FOR YOU TO ENJOY

SHOTWELLPUBLISHING.COM

JEFFERY ADDICOTT
Union Terror: Debunking the False Justifications for Union Terror

Trampling Union Terror: Riders of the Second Alabama Cavalry

MARK ATKINS
Women in Combat: Feminism Goes to War

JOYCE BENNETT
Maryland, My Maryland: The Cultural Cleansing of a Small Southern State

GARRY BOWERS
Slavery and The Civil War: What Your History Teacher Didn't Tell You

Dixie Days: Reminiscences Of a Southern Boyhood

JERRY BREWER
Dismantling the Republic

ANDREW P. CALHOUN
My Own Darling Wife: Letters From A Confederate Volunteer

JOHN CHODES
Segregation: Federal Policy or Racism?

Washington's KKK: The Union League During Southern Reconstruction

WALTER BRIAN CISCO
War Crimes Against Southern Civilians

DAVID T. CRUM
Stonewall Jackson: Saved by Providence

JOHN DEVANNY
Continuities: The South in a Time of Revolution

Lincoln's Continuing Revolution: Essays of M.E. Bradford and Thomas H. Landess

JOSHUA DOGGRELL
Doxed: The Political Lynching of a Southern Cop

JAMES C. EDWARDS
What Really Happened?: Quantrill's Raid On Lawrence, Kansas

TED EHMANN
Boom & Bust In Bone Valley: Florida's Phosphate Mining History 1886-2021

JOHN AVERY EMISON
The Deep State Assassination of Martin Luther King Jr.

DON GORDON
Snowball's Chance: My Kidneys Failed, My Wife Left Me & My Dog Died...

JOHN R. GRAHAM
Constitutional History of Secession

PAUL C. GRAHAM
Confederaphobia

When The Yankees Come: Former Carolina Slaves Remember

Nonsense on Stilts: The Gettysburg Address & Lincoln's Imaginary Nation

JOE D. HAINES
The Diary of Col. John Henry Stover Funk of the Stonewall Brigade, 1861-1862

CHARLES HAYES
The REAL First Thanksgiving

V.P. HUGHES
Col. John Singleton Mosby: In the News 1862-1916

TERRY HULSEY
25 Texas Heroes

*The Constitution of Non-State Government:
Field Guide to Texas Secession*

JOSEPH JAY
*Sacred Conviction:
The South's Stand for Biblical Authority*

JAMES R. KENNEDY
Dixie Rising: Rules For Rebels

*Nullifying Federal and State Gun Control:
A How-To Guide For Gun Owners*

*When Rebel Was Cool:
Growing Up In Dixie, 1950-1965*

*Reconstruction: Destroying the Republic
and Creating an Empire*

WALTER D. KENNEDY
The South's Struggle: America's Hope

*Lincoln, The Non-Christian President:
Exposing The Myth*

Lincoln, Marx, and the GOP

J.R. & W.D. KENNEDY
*Jefferson Davis: High Road to Emancipation
and Constitutional Government*

*Yankee Empire:
Aggressive Abroad and Despotic at Home*

Punished With Poverty: The Suffering South

The South Was Right! 3rd Edition

LEWIS LIBERMAN
Snowflake Buddies; ABC Leftism For Kids!

PHILIP LEIGH
*The Devil's Town: Hot Springs During
The Gangster Era*

U.S. Grant's Failed Presidency

The Causes of the Civil War

*The Dreadful Frauds: Critical Race Theory
And Identity Politics*

JACK MARQUARDT
*Around The World In 80 Years: Confessions
of a Connecticut Confederate*

MICHAEL MARTIN
Southern Grit: Sensing The Siege at Petersburg

SAMUEL MITCHAM
*The Greatest Lynching In American History:
New York, 1863*

*Confederate Patton: Richard Taylor and
The Red River Campaign*

CHARLES T. PACE
Lincoln As He Really Was

*Southern Independence. Why War? The War
To Prevent Southern Independence*

JAMES R. ROESCH
From Founding Fathers To Fire Eaters

KIRKPATRICK SALE
*Emancipation Hell: The Tragedy Wrought
By Lincoln's Emancipation Proclamation*

JOSEPH SCOTCHIE
*The Asheville Connection:
The Making of a Conservative*

ANNE W. SMITH
Charlottesville Untold: Inside Unite The Right

Robert E. Lee: A History for Kids

KAREN STOKES
A Legion Of Devils: Sherman In South Carolina

The Burning of Columbia, S.C.: A Review of Northern Assertions and Southern Facts

Carolina Love Letters

Fortunes of War: The Adventures of a German Confederate

A Confederate in Paris: Letters of A. Dudley Mann 1867-1879

JOSEPH R. STROMBERG
Southern Story and Song: Country Music in the 20th Century

JACK TROTTER
Last Train to Dixie

JOHN THEURSAM
Key West's Civil War

H.V. TRAYWICK, JR.
Along The Shadow Line: A Road Trip through History and Memory on the Old Confederate Border

LESLIE TUCKER
Old Times There Should Not Be Forgotten: Cultural Genocide In Dixie

JOHN VINSON
Southerner Take Your Stand!

MARK R. WINCHELL
Confessions of a Copperhead: Culture and Politics in the Modern South

CLYDE N. WILSON
Calhoun: A Statesman for the 21st Century

Lies My Teacher Told Me: The True History of the War For Southern Independence

The Yankee Problem: An American Dilemma

Annals Of The Stupid Party: Republicans Before Trump

Nullification: Reclaiming The Consent of the Governed

The Old South: 50 Essential Books

The War Between The States: 60 Essential Books

Reconstruction and the New South, 1865-1913: 50 Essential Books

The South 20th Century And Beyond: 50 Essential Books

Southern Poets and Poems, 1606 -1860: The Land They Loved, Volume 1

Confederate Poets and Poems, Vol 1 The Land They Loved, Volume II

Looking For Mr. Jefferson

African American Slavery in Historical Perspective

JOE WOLVERTON
What Degree Of Madness?: Madison's Method To Make American States Again

WALTER KIRK WOOD
Beyond Slavery: The Northern Romantic Nationalist Origins of America's Civil War

SHOTWELL
COLUMBIA · So. Car.
EST. 2015
PUBLISHING

SHOTWELLPUBLISHING.COM

Green Altar (Literary Imprint)

CATHARINE SAVAGE BROSMAN
An Aesthetic Education
and Other Stories (2nd Ed)

Chained Tree, Chained Owls: Poems

Aerosols and Other Poems

Partial Memoirs

RANDALL IVEY
A New England Romance:
And Other Southern Stories

The Gift of Gab

SUZANNE JOHNSON
Maxcy Gregg's Sporting Journals 1842-1858

JAMES E. KIBLER, JR.
Tiller : Claybank County Series, Vol. 4

The Gentler Gamester

In the Deep Heart's Core: Poems of Tribute and
Remembrance (forthcoming)

THOMAS MOORE
A Fatal Mercy:
The Man Who Lost The Civil War

PERRIN LOVETT
The Substitute, Tom Ironsides 1

KAREN STOKES
Belles

Carolina Twilight

Honor in the Dust

The Immortals

The Soldier's Ghost: A Tale of Charleston

WILLIAM THOMAS
Runaway Haley:
An Imagined Family Saga

The Field of Justice: Moonshine
and Murder in North Georgia

CLYDE N. WILSON
Southern Poets and Poems, 1606-1860:
The Land They Loved, Volume 1

Confederate Poets and Poems, Vol1
The Land They Loved, Volume II

Gold-Bug
(Mystery & Suspense Imprint)

BRANDI PERRY
Splintered: A New Orleans Tale

MARTIN WILSON
To Jekyll and Hide

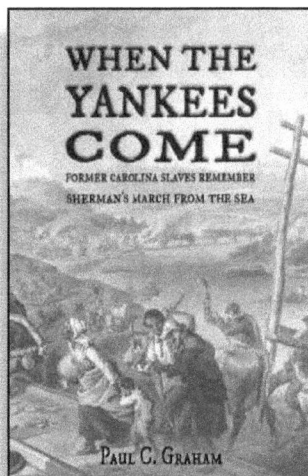